D1433915

ASPECTS OF GEOGRAPHY

General Editors: J. H. Johnson and Ian Douglas

Population Migration

JAMES H. JOHNSON

University of Lancaster

JOHN SALT

University College London

Nelson

Thomas Nelson and Sons Ltd
Nelson House Mayfield Road
Walton-on-Thames Surrey
KT12 5PL UK

Nelson Blackie
Wester Cleddens Road
Bishopbriggs
Glasgow
G64 2NZ UK

Thomas Nelson (Hong Kong) Ltd
Toppan Building 10/F
22a Westlands Road
Quarry Bay Hong Kong

Thomas Nelson Australia
102 Dodds Street
South Melbourne
Victoria 3205 Australia

Nelson Canada
1120 Birchmount Road
Scarborough Ontario
M1K 5G4 Canada

© J. H. Johnson and John Salt, 1992

First published by Thomas Nelson and Sons Ltd 19924

ISBN 0-17-448185-3
NPN 9 8 7 6 5 4 3

Printed in Singapore

Contents

Preface

1. The study of migration   1
2. Intra-urban migration   25
3. Internal migration   38
4. International migration   56

Project work   72
Bibliography and further reading   74

Preface

The *Aspects of Geography* series has been organised as a series of concise reports which attempt to provide easily accessible summaries of recent developments in geographical knowledge. The books in the series are aimed in particular at enquiring A-level students and their teachers, but it is hoped that they will also be useful to college and university students as an introduction to various specialist fields.

One repetitive characteristic of modern societies and economies is that population movements of various kinds grow more common and more complex. Changes in the location of permanent residences form the most important of these movements for many households; and these residential changes are commonly taken to constitute population migration. Population migration has various dimensions, ranging from simple, short-distance alterations in the location of homes to longer moves which also involve a search for new jobs and even changes of nationality. The aim of this book is to outline the various types of migration which occur in the modern world and to indicate some of their immediate implications.

Associated with the process of population migration has been an increased concentration of people in large cities. This, in turn, has further effects on the evolution of new kinds of social interaction, changes in family size and structure, alterations in the way political institutions operate, and the development of new methods by which innovations are diffused. Clearly these broader matters must lie beyond the scope of this short book, but it is important to notice that population migration is not only associated with these far-reaching social and economic changes, but that it is also one of the most important factors which have encouraged them to take place. Population is never static and at a variety of scales migration is a many-faceted influence on geographical change.

J.H. JOHNSON
IAN DOUGLAS

1 The study of migration

Types of Migration

As societies, economies and transport systems become modernised, more frequent, longer and more complex movements of population commonly take place. In England and Wales, for example, it is likely that over 1m households will move home every year and the United States census shows that there more than 91m people moved home between 1975 and 1980 (Table 1). Movements of populations have been classified in many ways, reflecting the complexities of the processes by which people are relocated. An important distinction, however, is between temporary movements connected with everyday activities and those moves which involve a change of home, with the social and economic impacts which this involves.

This does not infer that the two types are independent, since temporary movements often provide the opportunity to acquire the information which may eventually lead to longer-term migration. For example, retirement moves are often made to resort areas known earlier in life and residential moves within individual cities are frequently made to sectors of the city which are known to the migrants for other reasons.

However, the term *migration* is generally applied to movements that involve a change of home; and as this implies a permanent move – insofar as any population movement in a modern urban society can be called 'permanent' – migration is a significant force in the process of geographical change.

In detail, population migration can take place over a great variety of distances and for diverse reasons, but certain broad types of migration can be recognised. Figure 1 illustrates some types of migration in terms of the distance travelled and the length of time the migrant stays at his or her destination. It also serves to place permanent moves on the same diagram as temporary population changes of various kinds to which the term *circulation* is sometimes applied.

What the diagram makes clear is that in practice a clear distinction between permanent and temporary migration is difficult to make convincingly. For example, these days an annual holiday may involve an international movement, but although this may have important economic implications for the destination region it has less significant implications for the holiday-makers themselves, in the short run at

Location after 5 year interval	Total population (5 years old and over) in thousands	Per cent
In same house (i.e. non-migrants)	202,216	68.0
In different house (i.e. internal migrants)	91,146	30.7
In same SMSA	(41,619)	(14.0)
Moves between SMSAs	(14,551)	(4.9)
From outside SMSAs into SMSAs	(5,993)	(2.0)
From SMSAs to outside SMSAs	(7,337)	(2.5)
Outside SMSAs at both dates	(21,647)	(7.3)
Moves from abroad (i.e. immigration)	3,813	1.3
	297,175	100.0

Table 1 Mobility of US Population, March 1975–March 1980 (by Standard Metropolitan Statistical Area) (Source: US Bureau of the Census, *Geographical Mobility, March 1975 to March 1980,* Washington, 1981)

least. In contrast, movements for temporary employment may have much more profound effects on the migrants, as for example the movement of workers to the mines of South Africa from surrounding States. Indeed with workers of this kind it is often difficult to specify precisely where their permanent homes actually are, as they may spend longer away from their legal home areas than at their work locations.

In other cases temporary migration may represent a much less drastic change of location. For example, the now disappearing annual movements in the Alpine and Mediterranean regions of Europe,

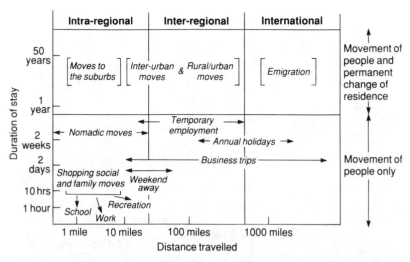

Figure 1 **A classification of population movements**

known as transhumance, served to extend the resource base of the home community by using land that was only available during certain times of the year and involved just a part of the population in tending livestock on seasonal pastures (Figure 2). Or again, temporary movements of harvest workers from Ireland to Britain in the nineteenth century also helped to maintain home communities, since these workers brought back a cash income, although these movements also introduced the seeds of change, by producing increased familiarity with areas away from home and hence tending to encourage permanent migration in the longer term.

When attention is turned to moves which can be more unequivocally defined as permanent migration, it is clear that most modern migration can be classified as *internal migration*, that is migration which occurs within the frontiers of individual nations. There are various ways of subdividing internal migration. One important distinction is between migration which involves merely a change of home (*residential migration*) and that which also involves a parallel change in employment (*labour migration*). Residential migration can result in distinctive residential areas within individual cities, while labour migration can produce relatively long-distance relocation of skills and thus has an important bearing on regional contrasts in economic change. Some caution must be used in interpreting these different

Figure 2 A nineteenth century silhouette representing Alpine transhumance.

This nineteenth century silhouette symbolises some features of transhumance in the Alps. Part of the rural population moved with their cattle and other livestock to the extra grazing lands that became available in summer when the snows melted on the higher Alps and returned again to the lower lands in the autumn. The regular movement was carefully tailored to the detailed topography and changing seasons of the mountains, but modern requirements of labour for tourism, resistance among younger people to the more primitive living conditions on the upland pastures, and changing demands for agricultural products have all led to its decline. It now only survives in a simplified and curtailed form.

types from census information. As Figure 3 illustrates, detailed distinctions in published statistics may sometimes owe more to the units by which migration information is gathered than to real geographical contrasts; but important differences underlie various genuine types of internal migration.

In the nineteenth century *international migration*, particularly from Europe to North America, was important. This kind of movement, which involves crossing a national border, still occurs, sometimes seen in the forced movement of refugees but also in the movement of workers between nations. International movements are

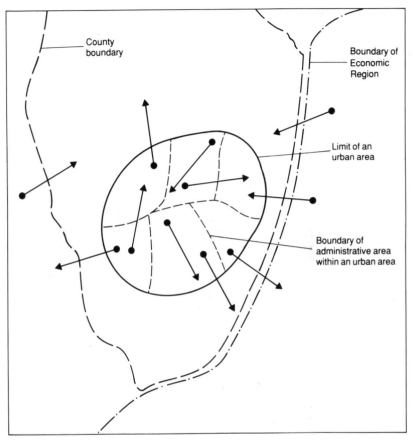

Figure 3 Internal population migration: problems in classification.

All the population moves on this hypothetical diagram are assumed for simplicity to cover exactly the same distance. Two do not cross any legal boundary and would thus not be recorded on a census return. Five cross the outer boundary of what is classified as an urban area and would therefore be considered to be either rural/urban or urban/rural moves. Another five cross a county boundary and could therefore be considered inter-county moves. Three cross the boundary of an economic region and might as a result be classified as inter-regional moves. Two cross local administrative boundaries within the urban area, thus representing intra-urban movement. However, in this particular hypothetical case it is likely that in fact they are all rather similar residential moves. Internal moves of different types certainly take place within nations, but some caution has to be exercised in interpreting census statistics, particularly when they refer to limited areas.

now commonly impeded by quotas and restrictions of various kinds. For example, in 1988 Canada raised its quota to 125–135 000. This figure was subdivided into various components, including 50 000 family members, 36–43 000 selected workers and their dependants and 21 000 refugees.

Highly skilled professional workers, however, are in such demand that national frontiers provide less impervious barriers to their movement than to workers of other kinds. In looking at movements of population across international boundaries it should be remembered that immigrants or emigrants represent only a small fraction of all the people who move internationally. Of nearly 8.5m passengers given leave to enter the United Kingdom in 1989 the vast majority were visitors, but others fell into a range of categories which are related to their likely length of stay (Table 2).

In most practical studies of migration a *migrant* is in fact someone who makes a move across an administrative boundary. Migration, of course, can take place within administrative areas, but unfortunately such local moves are often not recorded in official statistics. Some migrants return eventually to their places of origin and these *return migrants* will have been away from their original homes for a considerable period, measured in years rather than months.

When migrants move out of a national area they take part in *emigration* rather than *out-migration*, which occurs within a State. Those who move in from another country are involved *in immigration* rather than *in-migration*, which again occurs within a nation.

	(000s)
Total admitted	8,440
Visitors	6,230
In transit	752
Students and au pairs	183
Passengers returning	1,107
Working permit holders and dependants	30
Accepted for settlement on arrival	14
Others	124

Table 2 Passengers given leave in 1989 to enter the UK by purpose of journey (excluding EC)

Migration can be measured in a number of ways but it is necessary to make a distinction between *gross migration*, which includes all the migrants who move into or out of an area and *net migration*, which is the balance between the number of migrants who have moved into an area and those who have moved out. A group of migrants who have a common origin and destination area form a *migration stream*, but there is often a *counterstream* flowing in the opposite direction.

Migration data

The demographic equation
Information on migration is often derived from census reports and it is important to remember that this source of information has some severe limitations when population movements, as opposed to population totals, are being assessed. There are considerable gaps between censuses, often as long as ten years and sometimes longer, so that many changes which occur between censuses are imperfectly revealed. Migration is calculated from censuses in several ways. One starting point is to use what is called the 'demographic equation':

$$P(t) = P(t-1) + B(t-1, t) - D(t-1, t) + IM(t-1, t) - OM(t-1, t)$$

where

P(t) represents the population in an area at the last census, $P(t-1)$ represents the population at the immediately previous census, $B(t-1, t)$ is the number of people born between the last two censuses, $D(t-1, t)$ is the number who died in the same period, IM $(t-1, t)$ the number who migrated into the area during the same period and OM $(t-1, t)$ the number who migrated out between the censuses.

What this means simply is that the population in an area at a particular census date consists of the population at the previous census, plus all the children who have been born between the censuses, minus all those who have died. To this total must be added all those who have migrated in, and all those who have migrated out must also be subtracted. This equation can be applied at a range of scales. In the world as a whole migration will not be relevant, at least not until space travel becomes a significant element in human activity. At the other extreme, say in a new housing estate, migration will be the completely dominant factor involved in population change.

Normally, however, migration will have an importance between these two extremes and, all other things being equal, the smaller the area involved the more important migration is likely to be.

Indirect assessment of migration

In many censuses migration has to be assessed indirectly from census statistics using this demographic equation. The total population at two successive census dates is known. If there is a proper system of recording vital statistics, which involves the registration of all births and deaths as they occur, it is possible to establish birth and death rates and to calculate what the population should have been at the time of the last census if migration had not occurred. This figure is then compared with the actual population returned at the last census, and if the actual figure is higher than expected then the amount of in-migration is revealed, and if it is lower then the amount of out-migration is shown. (See Table 3 for an example.)

	Population change	Natural increase	Net migration
1926-36	-3,572	163,179	-166,751
1936-46	-13,313	173,798	-187,111
1946-51*	5,486	125,054	-119,568
1951-56*	-62,329	135,434	-196,763
1956-61*	-79,923	132,080	-212,003
1961-66*	+65,661	146,266	-80,605
1966-71*	+94,246	148,152	-53,906
1971-81	+465,157	361,268	+103,889
1981-86*	+97,238	169,123	-71,885
1986-91*	-17,242	119,200	-136,442
*Five-year period			

Table 3 **Republic of Ireland – migration, natural increase and population change**

(In this table net migration in the Irish Republic is calculated from the total population change and the number of births and deaths registered in each intercensal period. The intercensal periods are either of 10 years or 5 years and this should be recalled in examining the statistics. The resulting figure for migration is a net figure, and this hides more substantial flows both into and out of the Irish Republic. Nor is natural increase independent of migration, since those who move are often young adults in the child-bearing age groups. Note in particular the sharp rise in natural increase in the period from 1971 to 1981, produced by the fact that fewer people in this age group were leaving Ireland and also that some were probably returning, as this was a period of net in-migration.)

Several difficulties with this method are obvious.

1 The accuracy of the result depends on the reliability of the records of deaths and births; and these in fact vary greatly in their dependability in different parts of the world.

2 Only net migration (the difference between the total amount of in-migration and out-migration) can be calculated in this way and substantial movements may well be hidden, particularly if in-migration and out-migration are roughly in balance.

3 Migration is only captured as a net change over the whole inter-censal period, but fluctuations from year to year, which might be associated with important economic and social changes, are also hidden.

Direct records of migration

Some censuses, however, ask a specific question or questions about migration. The US census, for example, simply asks 'Did you live in the same house five years previously or did you live elsewhere?' A question of this kind allows gross migration (the total movement into and out of an area) to be appraised and it also allows calculation of the distance moved. In the US census, people who said that they lived elsewhere 5 years earlier are classified into 6 different types: whether they lived (1) in the same local political unit, (2) in the same Standard Metropolitan Statistical Area (roughly speaking, in the same major city), (3) in the same county, (4) in another county of the same State, (5) in another State in the USA, or (6) abroad. A simplified and summary version of the results for the period 1975 to 1980 is presented in Table 1. As a result movements of varying levels of apparent distance can be studied, although it should be noted that the classification procedure imposes a hierarchical arrangement on the data, which may or may not coincide with detailed geographical reality. For example, migration within a large county may be over a longer distance than movement between States, depending on the precise location of administrative boundaries. Figure 3 presents a hypothetical situation to illustrate in simple form some of the problems that might arise with movements in and around a large city.

There are other difficulties with this kind of information. During a period of 5 years some particularly mobile households may move their homes a number of times, so it is difficult to make a valid interpretation of their answers. In an extreme case they may have moved out of and back into the same area, thus escaping record in the statistics. Further, the longer the period over which a household is asked to recall its past migration, the more likely it is that mistakes will be made in remembering just when and where particular moves were made. For example, the British censuses of 1966 and 1971 asked a question about the location of householders 5 years earlier, but there have been considerable doubts about the validity of the answers received. It is probably more reliable to use information from a less ambitious question which simply asks where the members of a household lived one year earlier. In Britain this latter question was asked in 1981 (and at every census since 1961) but the 5-year question has now been dropped.

Itinerants

In any country there are always some migrants whose pattern of movement is short-term and/or irregular. As a result their patterns of life are rarely captured by censuses. Traditionally those engaged in transhumance, pastoral nomadism, gypsies and other travellers come into this category, although the underlying social and economic implications of these various movements are clearly very different. The number of these people is now much lower and is continuing to fall. Seasonal work in agriculture still requires some migrant workers, but the large gangs of workers who used to take on such tasks as harvesting hops, vines and potatoes or hoeing sugar beet and turnips are now much diminished, thanks to mechanisation. Seasonal workers, many of them migrants, are still required in the hotel and catering industry, their employment being made easier by the provision in many cases of accommodation with the job. In some countries people move between summer and winter tourist resorts, from seaside to mountains, following the recreations practised in different seasons.

A major employer of itinerant workers has traditionally been the construction industry. In the nineteenth century gangs of navvies built canals and railways. They have their modern-day counterparts. Projects like the Channel Tunnel, the construction of new motorways or large power stations require thousands of workers, for whom the job finishes when the project is complete. They then move to another major project in a new location. In Britain many construction workers live in cheap lodgings during the week, travelling home to their families only at weekends. Often construction project work is international; many European companies, for example, employ their own nationals (as well as those of other countries) in the Middle East on work of this kind.

One special group of itinerants is made up of students. In any year many new students move to centres of higher education. Where there is a tradition of leaving home for higher education the geography of student migration differs from that of other groups. A study in the United Kingdom of a sample of 69,631 students found that those who left home moved an average distance to university of 193 km. This migratory tendency among large numbers of a nation's intellectual young has important implications for future migration. Propensity to migrate increases the more moves a person makes. By getting on the migration train at an early age, and by breaking many of the social ties with the home region, it becomes easier to contemplate a new move in the future and to carry it through. In this way the British system of higher education may encourage future labour mobility.

Motives for Migration

Although there are considerable difficulties in establishing the basic facts about population migration because of the nature of the available data, much greater problems arise when explanation of migration is attempted. The obvious solution would seem to be simply to ask migrants why they have moved, using a social survey of some kind. Table 4 provides an example of the results of such a survey.

Problems in social surveys

Yet things are rarely as simple as they seem. To start with, because migrants by definition are people who have recently moved home it is not always easy to establish their addresses in order to conduct a survey. Even if, by careful comparison of registers of householders from different dates, it is possible to compile a list of migrants, by the time that a survey can be conducted considerable time may have passed since they actually moved home. As a result the precise reasons for moving to a particular location are likely to have faded in the minds of the migrants and been replaced by new information which has been acquired since the move, rather than known at the times when the actual decision to move was being made. In any case, when questioned by an outside enquirer householders are often anxious to make their migration behaviour seem sensible and beneficial, since otherwise they would be presenting themselves as having made a silly decision.

As a result it might seem desirable to interview migrants before they actually move, in order to gain a more valid insight into the reason for migration. Such advice represents an unattainable counsel of

	Chatham	High Wycombe	Hudders-field	North-hampton	Total
	%	%	%	%	%
Job reasons	41.3	53.4	51.3	50.3	49.4
Setting up business	2.4	2.3	5.3	1.2	2.4
Housing reasons	15.1	5.1	4.0	18.1	11.3
'Home town'	16.7	10.1	21.1	11.1	13.4
'Liked area'	4.8	9.6	2.6	6.4	6.5
Personal reasons	7.9	5.6	7.9	4.1	6.0
Travelling time	11.9	12.4	4.0	8.2	9.8
Other	–	1.6	4.0	0.6	1.3

Table 4 **Reasons given by labour migrant households for moving into four contrasting towns in England and Wales (Source: Johnson, Salt and Wood 1974)**

Although the principal wage-earner in each of these households had moved his or her job as well as home, the acquisition of a job was far from the only reason for moving. The survey identified a surprising range of unprompted reasons for labour migration and only half of the sample household moved specifically for employment reasons (including the setting up of businesses).

perfection, since it is almost impossible to find a valid sample of migrants before they have moved. Even when ingenious detection work makes it possible to interview some migrants before they have left their original homes there remain considerable problems in establishing the true reasons for moving.

To start with, a migrant household often consists of more than one person, so that in many cases some sort of joint decision involving a contribution from all the members of a household is likely to have been made. For instance, in families where both parents are in paid employment and children are attending school, the needs of any one person in the household may take precedence at various times. As a result the best that is likely to be obtained is an individual perception of why the household plans to move, rather than an objective assessment of the factors behind a joint decision. Even more difficult is the fact that the reasons an individual gives for moving usually reflect his or her immediate personal stimulation for choosing a destination or for leaving an area, since the underlying economic, social and economic processes involved are often left unstated, and are perhaps not always fully comprehended by the individuals involved. Regional contrasts in economic growth, longer-term opportunities for upward social mobility, the need for the out-migration of siblings in a system of family farming if economic farm units are to be maintained, the existence of a repressive social system in which initiative is undervalued – these are examples of the kind of factor which is often taken for granted. When migrants are questioned these more wide-ranging considerations are left on one side and are replaced by more immediate reasons for moving – like the possibility of obtaining a particular job, the chance of joining a near relative already established elsewhere, the decision to marry someone in another community, or vague general ideas about seeking the 'bright lights' in a growing city.

One response to this problem is to use statistical analyses of various kinds to discover a connection between the amount of migration and the incidence of other social and economic features in the areas under study. One difficulty is that such approaches often depend on seeing migration as being the product of a 'push' from the departure area and a 'pull' from the destination area. Although this is one possible explanatory framework for emigration it is not the only one that can be envisaged and this will be discussed later. In any case, the 'push' or 'pull' often consists of collections of factors of different levels of importance, rather than one simple cause.

There are also considerable problems in extracting conclusions about migration from aggregate statistical data, since migrants usually form only a small part of the total population in any one year and they are likely to have distinctive characteristics of their own. As a result there is a danger in assuming that the general economic conditions in an area are what motivate migration, when in fact migration may be encouraged by more specific factors which affect only the migrants and not the population as a whole.

Characteristics of migrants

This problem is made more difficult by the fact that contrasting types of migration are likely to be made up of migrants who show different personal characteristics and have distinctive reasons for moving. These will be explored in later sections of this book, but there are some general observations that can be made about the nature of migrants, particularly about those found in the advanced economies.

One obvious feature is the age of the migrants. With the exception of retirement migration, which represents a special case and gives an impetus to movement among people in their 60s, most migrants are young adults, often between the ages of 20 and 35. Quite young children are also found in migration streams, since they are moving with their parents, but a large family often acts as a check to migration not only because of the costs involved, but also because of the deep and diverse social ties which an established family will have built up with a local community. The impact of the family life-cycle is most clearly seen in intra-urban residential migration and will be discussed in more detail later in this book, but life-cycle considerations influence migration of all kinds.

Age is not the only consideration. The differences between the overall migration rates of men and women are not usually too great in the modern world, although there is some evidence that in the past women have been more likely to be involved in short distance migration and men in longer distance moves. Men dominated the temporary movement of harvest workers in the nineteenth century and they still completely dominate moves associated with temporary employment on large civil engineering projects. Women, however, are more important in moves to temporary employment in the service industries of modern western cities. This is true in the Third World as well. A growing number of women in the Middle East are moving internationally to work as house maids, for example from Sri Lanka to the Gulf States. In the Far East many young women are migrating to work in a range of service industries, including employment as bar maids and prostitutes as well as more conventional activities. With exceptions like these, most modern migration consists of men and women in roughly equal numbers.

A further comment is to do with the standing in society of those who move. A simple view is that out-migrants are driven out of their homes by poverty. In some cases this is undoubtedly true, but more often out-migrants are a section of the population with more initiative than average. Even in nineteenth century Ireland, characterised by mass emigration to North America, emigrants had at least sufficient resources to find the fare needed to emigrate and they were frequently not the poorest in the community, with the possible exception of the period of the Great Famine in the 1840s. The more highly educated a person is, the more probable it is that he or she will become a migrant. For example, in the United States people with a college education are six times more likely to move to an adjoining state than those who have only been educated to an elementary level. This feature may be true in the less developed countries as well.

Approaches to migration analysis

Given these complexities, it is not easy to know how best to generalise about the causes and spatial patterns of migration. Over the last century, many theories have been developed and used, most of which have their roots in the pioneering work of Ravenstein who, in the 1880s, produced the first attempt to formalise migration behaviour into a set of 'laws'.

Ravenstein's laws of migration (see Figure 4) were initially based on his observations of migration patterns in Great Britain, supplemented later by data from North America. Despite their antiquity now, his ideas continue to have validity, for he developed a set of concepts which still condition much of our thinking about why people move and where they go. Particularly important are the laws which state that most migrants move short distances, that large centres exert greater attractive power than smaller ones, that for every flow there is a counter-flow, and that economic reasons underlie most migrations.

Since the time of Ravenstein the development of theories to explain why people migrate has been characterised by three approaches: ecological, behavioural and systems. These should be regarded as complementary rather than competing ways of thinking,

---

1. Most migrants go short distances
2. Migration proceeds step by step
3. Longer-distance migrants prefer to go to great centres of commerce or industry
4. Each stream of migration produces a compensation counter-stream
5. Urban dwellers are less migratory than people in rural areas
6. Females are more migratory than males in intenral migration, but males are more common in international migration
7. Most migrants are adults; families rarely migrate out of their country of birth
8. Large towns owe more of their growth to migration than to natural increase
9. The volume of migration increase with the development of industry and commerce and as transport improves
10. Most migration is from the agricultural areas to centres of industry and commerce
11. The major causes of migration are economic

Figure 4 **Ravenstein's Laws of Migration (originally from 1880s)**

since each has something to offer, depending upon the specific questions about migration we want to answer.

Ecological theories

The ecological approach to migration emphasises the importance of the characteristics of origin and destination places in the decision to move. Perhaps the best known ecological model is the gravity model, which in its most simple form is expressed as $Mij = PiPj/D$. What this says is that migration between origin i and destination j is proportional to the size of the two places, Pi and Pj, but inversely related to the distance between them. In other words, more migration will take place between large places than small places, and there will be less movement the greater distance that the two places are apart. Easily recognisable here are Ravenstein's laws 1 and 3.

The way we measure size and distance in the gravity model may be varied. Rather than simply using population totals as an indication of size, it may be better to use the number of workers, or, if we are interested in particular types of movers, the relevant numbers of those people. An example would be the size of the population aged over 60 or 65 for a study of retirement migration. Distance can also be measured in several ways: in a straight line or by road; in some cases time or cost would be more appropriate measures.

It was the problem of choosing the best measure of distance that persuaded Stouffer to suggest using the number of 'intervening opportunities', that is the number of alternative destinations within a given distance of the origin. We can see how this works in Figure 5. A person at i, thinking of moving to j, might also consider other destinations within the circle of radius i-j, providing there was no difference in the cost of moving. In a later model Stouffer introduced the idea of 'competing migrants', this time using i-j as the diameter of the circle. The principle was that a person from i, wishing to go to j, would be in competition for jobs, housing, etc, from others contemplating the same course of action.

The gravity model can be extended by incorporating other variables which say something about what places are like. Unemployment and wage rates are frequently used, especially by economists, on the assumption that those without jobs may get on their bikes and move to places where employment is available. Social variables such as housing characteristics, amount of open space or other measures of environmental quality can also be incorporated into regression models, depending upon what aspects of places we think are likely to be

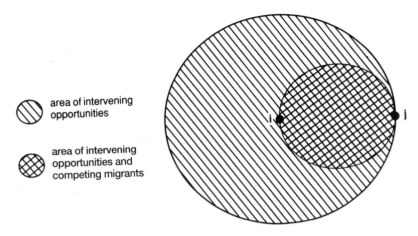

area of intervening opportunities

area of intervening opportunities and competing migrants

Figure 5 Stouffer's models of intervening opportunities and competing migrants

important in persuading people to migrate.

The weakness of ecological models is that they concentrate upon places rather than people. They assume that everyone will make a similar and rational response to place-specific stimuli, and that rationality is essentially economic. It is the need to consider migrants as individuals, not necessarily responding in the same way, that has given rise in recent decades to a more behavioural approach. This does not mean that the ecological approach now has no role; far from it. Its main strength now is to summarise the main relationships, say between depressed and prosperous areas, and suggest what other variables ought to be considered. By summarising movement between places in the form of a set of equations, it also allows forecasts to be made of future flows.

The behavioural approach

During the 1960s migration studies began to focus more on the factors inducing human behaviour, in this case the decision to move. It could no longer be assumed that people behaved like robots, automatically moving in response to broad forces which were themselves largely determined by place characteristics.

Wolpert, an American geographer, divided the decision to move into two phases – the assessment of place utility and search behaviour. He suggested that people considering a move would first assess the value of the place in which they lived. Only if there was real dissatisfaction and if alternative locations seemed likely to offer better opportunities would the next phase be entered. In this, potential migrants search for likely destinations and investigate their attractions. Whether and where people move depends upon how they look for alternative destinations and what sort of opportunities are sought there. Different sorts of people search in different ways, depending upon prior knowledge of alternative destinations and the sources of information known about them. In general, more highly educated and skilled migrants scan wider horizons and are more likely to move longer distances than those with lower levels of education and skill.

However, not everyone perceives comparative opportunities in the same way. Lee, an American sociologist, elaborated on Ravenstein's ideas in his 'dragon's teeth' model shown in Figure 6. Within the origin and destination areas are various place characteristics that might attract migrants (the pluses) or repel them (the minuses). These include such features as employment conditions, housing availability, climate and open space. However, the perception of these characteristics differs between migrants. For example, if you are an owner-occupier the availability of council houses in a potential destination may not be important, whereas if you are a local authority tenant the reverse might be the case. Some people find living in city centres attractive and exciting, to others such places are cramped and depressing. Response to isolation also varies, perhaps psychologically, perhaps depending upon whether you have a car and can drive. Hence there is no automatic response to place characteristics. How those characteristics are valued, and place utility calculated, may be perceived differently by different people.

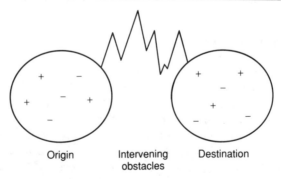

Figure 6 Lee's behavioural model of migration

But even if personal or household evaluation of places favours a move, there may still be intervening obstacles – the 'teeth' in the diagram. These obstacles are more or less easy to overcome, depending on the abilities and position of the individual or household. High house prices at the destination may be no deterrent to the rich, but of major importance to the less-well-off. Until recently, the Berlin Wall was a major intervening obstacle, crossed only with difficulty, unless, that is, you were a member of the communist élite.

Thus the essence of the behavioural approach is to put the emphasis on the migrant, not the place, when trying to understand why people move. It invokes the norms and values of the society in which people live and which influence the importance they attach to particular place characteristics. To some extent this allows us to argue that groups classified by age, occupation, family status, for example, will behave in similar fashion, but differently from other discrete groups. It also allows us to assume that some individuals may not respond exactly to group norms but to their own inclinations when confronting the decision to move and where to go.

The systems approach

Decisions about moving are made by individuals affected by the socio-economic, cultural and political contexts in which they find themselves. Their actions are influenced by factors which operate at a wide variety of scales, like the national and international economic situation, local physical and socio-economic conditions. They are also affected by a wide range of institutional structures such as building society policy on mortgage lending or government immigration policy. Migration is thus part of a system of interrelated elements. It also takes place in a particular historical context. Examples are the 'navvies' who came from Ireland to Great Britain in the nineteenth century to dig canals and build railways, or the Turks who responded to the labour needs of the German economic miracle in the 1960s. The effects of this historical context may linger on long after the original reasons for movement have ceased due to the links created – a form of chain migration.

One of the best known examples of a systems approach to migration is that of Mabogunje (Figure 7). It was originally developed to study rural-urban migration in Africa, but can easily be adapted to apply to other forms of migration and in other places. Mabogunje's approach views migration as part of an integrated complex of variables. In his system, the potential migrant leaves the rural area to become an urban dweller ('urbanite'). This takes places within a changing rural economy that is becoming less self-sufficient and more integrated into the national economy. Greater ease of communication makes rural people more aware of opportunities in growing urban centres. Government policies play an increasingly important role in the whole development process.

Within this framework Mabogunje identifies three main elements. First there are the potential migrants whose moves from their rural origins are influenced by environmental considerations. Second there are the two control sub-systems which consist of the package of institutional and societal influences which may encourage or hold back movement and make it easier or more difficult to settle at urban destinations. Finally there are adjustment mechanisms. In rural areas these help local economies and communities adjust to the loss of those who have left, while at urban destinations changes are made to accommodate new arrivals. Energy for the system is provided by the stimuli acting upon the individuals to move; the explanation of why people move is then seen in terms of differential responses to the stimuli, both from the external environment and from within the system. The migrants themselves play an important role by sending back information on their experiences to other potential migrants through feedback channels. Those who have been successful are more likely to be positive about the effect of the move upon them; the unsuccessful ones may well return and thus deter others from following their example. However, many who make a wrong move do not like to admit failure and send home more positive signals than they really feel.

This particular system has been described in detail as an illustration of the approach. In fact much contemporary interest in migration sees the need to view it in systems terms which reflect the total context in which migration occurs. The framework is capable of widespread adaptation beyond the rural-urban case to other types of migration. Furthermore, it does not only help in understanding causes of movement, but the consequences too, both for the individuals involved and for the communities they leave and join. It can also be argued that the movements not only respond to the sorts of environmental influences in Mabogunje's model, but that they in turn bring about changes in the environment. For example, rural areas may adjust to population loss by changes in agricultural practice, leading to new forms of production and marketing; or in areas of rapid foreign immigration, habitual tolerance may give way to chauvinism and xenophobia.

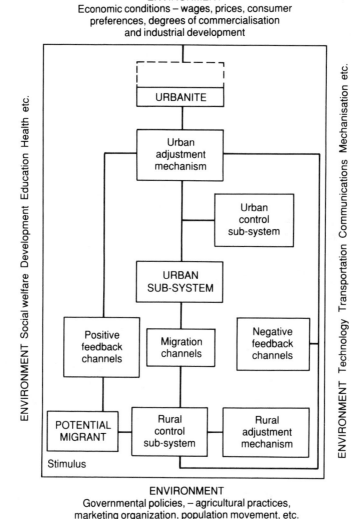

Figure 7 Mabogunje's Systems Model of Rural-Urban Migration

Recent approaches to migration study have moved away from emphasising differences between places to focusing on individuals and groups who display similar characteristics. This does not mean that the attributes of places are no longer important; indeed, looking at the sorts of places that attract and repel migrants can give us important clues as to why people behave as they do. In addition, we often want to know, for purposes of population forecasting, for example, what geographical patterns of movement are associated with particular places. But migration occurs in a wider temporal, spatial and institutional context; it is part of a system. If one element in the system changes, there are likely to be knock-on effects on the patterns and processes of movement, although it cannot be assumed that every individual or household will react in a similar way to that change.

The concept of the mobility transition

It is also necessary to look at migration in a much broader historical perspective. Wilbur Zelinsky has suggested that there have been regular patterns in the growth of personal mobility (and hence of population migration) in recent history. His ideas embrace both migration and various forms of less permanent movements of population like the journey to work and to recreation, to which the term 'circulation' has been applied. Zelinsky believes that there has been a *mobility transition*, which has run parallel to the more widely recognised 'demographic transition' – an idea which attempts to link the reductions over time in mortality and in fertility which have successively been found in many regions, starting with the industrialised countries of the western world, and possibly spreading eventually to other regions.

According to Zelinsky (Figure 8) the mobility transition is made up of five stages, related to parallel social and economic changes.

1. In a pre-modern traditional society there is little residential migration and limited circulation, set in the context of relatively stable total population numbers, high death rates and relatively high birth rates.

2. A second 'early transitional' stage then occurs, marked by a slight increase in fertility and also by the commencement of a long period of decline in mortality, thus producing rapid population increase. This period is marked by considerable rural-urban migration and the colonisation of new lands, with the associated growth of longer-distance migration (often in the form of emigration), and increased circulation.

3. In a third stage rates of natural increase gradually decelerate as birth rates begin to decline, but population increase continues, if more slowly than in the past. Rural-urban movements continue and

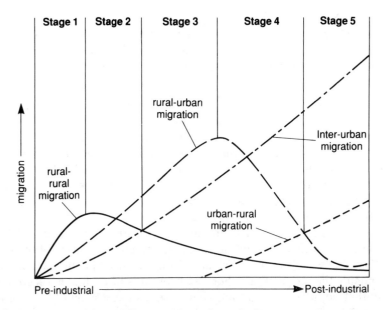

Figure 8 Aspects of the mobility transition (After Zelinsky, 1971, and Jones, 1990).

In Zelinsky's idea of mobility transition not only does the amount of migration change in the context of evolving rates of fertility and mortality (see text), but the types of migration found also vary in importance.

there is a rapid rise in migration between cities. Emigration is reduced, but various forms of circulation increase in size and complexity.

4. A fourth stage is found in an advanced society, where natural increase is limited as a result of a sharp decrease in fertility rates, which then tend to oscillate at low levels. The reduction in mortality also levels off, with the death rate becoming stable at a much lower level than in the past. Rural-urban migration may continue, but at a greatly reduced rate. Residential migration remains high, but is expressed in migration within and between cities, rather than in emigration or rural-urban migration. However, there may be immigration of unskilled workers, and highly trained professional workers – small in number but economically significant – may be exchanged between countries as a result of the operations of multi-national companies.

5. Finally, Zelinsky looks towards a hypothetical fifth stage in the future, where in some super-advanced societies residential migration will be almost exclusively inter-urban or intra-urban, although it is possible that new technology will reduce the need for migration somewhat and that there may also be less need for some types of circulation, like long-distance journeys-to-work. Mobility between and within countries might be rather strictly controlled by the State.

This is just simply a model and details vary in different areas. Although the generality of some of the descriptive points may be debated, what the idea of the mobility transition implies is that important social and economic changes underlie the various population movements which will be considered in the later chapters of this book. The developments the model seeks to summarise involve an increasing concentration of population in large cities, which in turn has further implications; for example, for the evolution of new kinds of social interaction, changes in family size and structure, alterations in the way political institutions operate, and the development of new methods by which innovations are diffused. These phenomena must lie outside the scope of this short book, but it is important to recall not only that population migration is an obvious expression of far-reaching social and economic changes, but also that it is one of the important processes which have allowed these changes to take place.

2 Intra-urban migration

Most permanent population migration is over relatively short distances and involves merely a change of home, rather than an accompanying change of job. This movement is generally called 'intra-urban' migration, although it might be more accurate to call it 'residential' migration, as it is a process which takes place in the countryside as well as in the town. In urban areas, however, short-distance migration is significant in that it provides the mechanism by which distinctive residential areas emerge, each characterised by a particular combination of age and social structure.

New urban housing tends to be built in estates which often consist of almost identical dwellings, each costing roughly the same, and it is therefore not surprising that to start with similar types of people come to live in these residential areas. As time passes change is likely to take place because other factors alter the relative attraction of these houses for particular groups. For example, larger houses originally designed for occupation by middle-class families and managed with the aid of servants have become less appropriate for modern life-styles, and have been subdivided to provide homes for smaller households, sometimes more mobile working class groups. In bringing about changes of this kind intra-urban migration is a critical factor.

Migration tends to affect families at certain stages in their lives, so that the people who move to and from particular locations are likely to belong to distinctive age and social groups. Access to private housing of different types depends on the level of wealth or credit worthiness possessed by a household; or the possibility of renting publicly-owned housing depends on meeting various formal criteria laid down by housing administrators. Again, these filters encourage the selective movement of similar people into particular types of housing.

The family life cycle and residential moves

The migration of a household is often examined as if it were an individual event, but in fact a move of home forms part of a sequence of occurrences which together form the life histories of the members of the household. The classic example of this is the family life cycle and its effects on residential mobility. Many residential moves of individuals are associated with different stages in their lives, starting as a young single person and ending, perhaps, as an elderly retired widow or widower. A household proceeds through various stages in this life

Stage in cycle	Access to specialised urban facilities	Space	Tenure	Mobility	Locational preference
Pre-child	Important	Unimportant	Rent flat	1-move	Near centre
Child-bearing	Less important	Growing importance	Rent house	2–3 moves	Middle and outer rings of central city
Child-rearing	Not important	Important	Own	1 move to owned house	Relatively new house in periphery or suburbs
Child-launching	Not important	Very important	Own	1 move to larger home	Suburbs or larger satellite town
Post-child	Not important	Less important	Own	1 move or no move	Possible move to more central location
Later life	Not important	Unimportant	Give up home	1 move	Perhaps closer to adult children or into sheltered accommodation

Table 5 **Life cycle and urban location**

cycle and at each stage the characteristics and the location of the residential accommodation that it requires tend to change (Table 5).

In the early years of their lives children are tied to the location of their parents' homes, automatically moving when they relocate. Eventually there comes a time when adult children leave home. Formerly this first step might have been at the time of their marriage, but today it is more likely that they will seek a life of their own earlier than this, perhaps moving away to their first jobs, or to obtain education away from home, or merely to enjoy the independence of a place of their own. A likely second step is to live with a partner, probably requiring more space and hence a move of home. If children are born, a couple is likely to make another move, again because of the pressure of space. As a new family grows older more living room will be required as possessions accumulate and demands on space expand.

For some this may introduce a period of relative stability but, in turn, their own children will eventually leave home and it may be that a more compact house would then be more appropriate. These days divorce is more common, with again a relocation being involved when a household breaks up. When the time for retirement arrives there may be a desire to reduce costs or to find a more easily managed home. The death of a partner may also encourage a move of home; or ill-health may demand a move to some more sheltered form of housing, where care of some kind can be provided.

Individual cases, of course, may not exactly fit this simple model. Marriage and a family are not the inevitable path that is chosen by all; remarriage may produce a recombination of step-children within households; the early death or long survival of a partner can distort the idealised progress that has been described. Nevertheless, the successive stages in the life cycle are probably the most important influences in generating residential moves.

These stages also have various implications for the location of residence. For example, at an early stage a single bed-sitting room may provide a home for a young independent person, but these small rented dwelling units tend to be located in inner parts of cities, where older properties are suitable for subdivision and are available for rent. The first home of a married couple might be a reasonably cheap rented flat, again less commonly located in the more affluent suburbs. However, if a young and growing family can afford a new home this is likely to be found in the suburbs. Or again, a couple with growing children may look for a location which provides access to a good school; and this may take precedence over easy access to the facilities of a town centre. If children have grown up sufficiently for both parents to go to work, then the cost and time of their combined journeys to work may play an important role in their choice of location. Retirement may encourage a move nearer to grown-up children. Clearly the locational possibilities for an individual are even more complex than the factors encouraging a move of home, but Table 5 attempts to bring together some of these ideas in tabular form. The locational and tenure changes indicated are rather more speculative than the suggested life cycle changes, which are probably more inevitable for most people and are less influenced than tenure and location by the characteristics of local housing markets.

External pressures to move

Life cycle changes may be seen as internal forces within a household that encourage migration; but there are also external forces which may encourage dissatisfaction with present housing. It is usual to see labour migration, in which people change their jobs and their homes at the same time, as being concerned with longer-distance migration between separate urban settlements; but in larger cities a change of job within the city may impose such an inconvenient journey to work that a move of home rapidly follows. Or again, as a household acquires more wealth it may feel that it wishes to move in order to give a visible expression of its increased financial status by living in a more affluent neighbourhood. Such a move may involve a change of tenure. For example, Table 7 (p.36) shows that in Great Britain about 16 per cent of new mortgages for house purchase were granted to people who were currently renting their homes.

A change of tenure is very likely to produce a change of location: a family living in a publicly-owned home may decide to purchase a house of its own; and this change of tenure also produces the need to move, except perhaps where local authority houses are for sale to existing tenants. Or the existing neighbourhood may change in various ways. For example, social change may take place: a contrasting ethnic group may colonise a local residential area and, if such a change is perceived as undesirable by the present residents, they may decide to move home if they have the necessary resources. The stimulus may be much more particular – a noisy neighbour or a deteriorating school may be sufficient to stimulate a family move. Nor need the move be voluntary. A road widening scheme or a commercial development can lead to houses being demolished and rehousing will then become necessary. Even if developments of this kind do not require the actual demolition of homes, they may make the local environment a much less attractive place in which to live.

It is sometimes convenient to classify moves in order to gain some impression of the relative importance of the causes of movement. In practice this is difficult, partly because of problems involved in gathering valid information about motives. Often more than one reason influences a decision to move: for example, life cycle changes may produce an increasing lack of fit between the needs of a family and the facilities provided by a house, but some specific external event, like a change of neighbour, triggers the decision to move. Or again, moves that might be explained by deficiences in the design of the current house may only be brought to the surface as a result of life cycle changes. In fact, when asked, the people who made the actual decision to move may find it difficult to recall the precise reason. It is nevertheless helpful to attempt to distinguish between *adjustment*, *induced* and *forced* moves. Adjustment moves include those which take place because of dissatisfaction with current housing characteristics, with the nature of the neighbourhood or with accessibility to work and services. Induced moves are a result of a specific change in employment, or in family size or structure. Forced moves occur where a household has no choice in the matter, as for example when slum clearance takes place.

As well as wanting to leave a particular place a household will also have another set of reasons for selecting the new location to which it moves. Many of the motives for choosing an area in which to live simply mirror the reasons for leaving the place of origin. Such factors include the availability of suitable housing for the changing needs of the family, the existence of residential areas which are deemed to have high status, and the possibility of finding a new location which will produce a less oppressive journey to work. In passing it should be noted that there is an interesting problem in interpreting access to work. Although a number of analyses of the structure of cities stress the importance of the journey to work and suggest that residential location is the result of a trade-off between a household's wish to live close to work and yet obtain acceptable levels of space and amenity, in fact when householders are questioned about their moves not many cite increased accessibility to work as the reason for relocating their homes. The assumption must be that the journey to work is not of prime importance until it reaches some critical level of time and cost. In addition, accessibility to work is only one of the various kinds of accessibility that are important to householders and the ability to reach such facilities as recreation, attractive shops and good schools also forms part of the more complex locational calculation that is made.

Information and residential migration

A problem which any household planning to move inevitably comes up against is that of putting together sufficient information to form a basis for decision making. Once a decision to move has been made the next step is to search for a new home (Figure 9). This involves choosing an area (or areas) in which to search. Statistically most moves are over a short distance, perhaps even to a destination only a few streets away. Just like other types of migration, distance acts as a constraint on movement, so that an analogy is frequently made with the operation of the force of gravity, and the 'gravity' models discussed in Chapter 1 can be successfully fitted to intra-urban migration statistics. It is usually assumed that the availability of information about alternative housing opportunities must be an important factor in producing this relationship. Quite simply, a household is more likely to know about suitable vacancies the closer to the point of origin these opportunities are located.

Residential movement also involves direction as well as distance. Within urban areas there is a tendency for the majority of moves to be made out towards the growing suburbs. This is not surprising, since this is the location of the sites for much new house building. It is also a location which offers more space for a growing family. Not all moves are in this direction, since single-person households and dual-income households without children may find housing more suitable for their needs closer to city centres. But as residential land use tends to be contracting in intensity in the inner city and expanding in the suburbs, the overall pattern of movement is still outwards. A diagrammatic summary of the situation in the larger metropolitan area of Britain in the late 1960s is given in Figure 10. Gross movements of population were both into and out of the various zones of the urban areas, but the net result was an outward relocation of population.

A further influence on the direction of movement is the particular sector of a city in which a migrant household originally resides. There is a tendency for households to move either outwards or inwards within a particular segment of a large city, rather than in a transverse direction. Again this pattern reflects the distribution of the information which a particular household is likely to have about housing opportunities. For example, if the wage-earners in a household work in the city centre it is their journey to work which will provide information about the residential characteristics of the sector that is traversed. Alternatively, repeated journeys to outdoor recreational facilities on the urban fringe or to suburban work-places may develop knowledge about residential opportunities at the edge of the city, but again it is likely that the areas known will be in the same general sector of the city in which the household already resides.

When a decision to move is made the situation changes somewhat, since a household's general awareness of the residential geography of

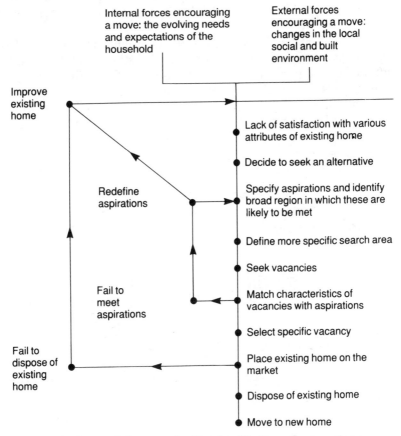

Figure 9 **Steps in the search for a new dwelling (Modified from Brown and Moore, 1970)**

its surroundings has to be converted to more specific information about the actual houses that are available. Not all the residential areas that the household is aware of will be inspected, since some will be eliminated because they are perceived as being undesirable. Others will be dropped because they do not meet the accessibility criteria of a particular household. Others will not be searched because it is believed that housing there is too expensive for the family budget. On the basis of these considerations, a smaller search area will be defined for more painstaking investigation. In a small city the search area may include a fairly comprehensive sample of all the acceptable housing opportunities available. The greater complexity of a large city will mean that here the search area is unlikely to cover all possibilities, simply because the household is not aware of the total residential geography of the urban area.

Having established a search area, the household will begin to look for vacant housing. There are a number of strategies which can be adopted. Newspaper advertisements, word-of-mouth information from friends, 'for sale' boards, information from council offices and estate agents can all be used (Table 6). The precise method is strongly influenced by the type of accommodation being sought. Most writers on this topic assume that a house is being purchased; and although sales are sometimes arranged between individuals, more often than not the service of an estate agent prove useful in bringing a purchase

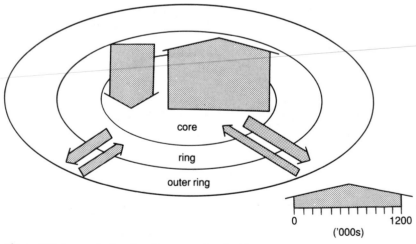

Figure 10 **Interzonal migration flows associated with metropolitan areas in Great Britain, 1966–70 (After Kennett, 1977)**

to completion, even if the agency was not the source of the original information about the availability of the house.

A further restriction on the search process is introduced here, since searching for housing involves a considerable investment of time. Sometimes a household considering a move gives up because it can find nothing better than its present home – or, at least, not sufficiently better to justify the cost and disruption of a move. In these circumstances a better strategy may be to consider making structural alterations to the existing dwelling. Alternatively the decision may be to take the matter no further at this stage, but at leisure to reconsider the nature and location of the accommodation that is to be searched for before starting the hunt again.

Similarly there is a limit to the amount of information about possible housing that it is possible to digest. As a result, a household is unlikely to find the 'best' new house in any objective sense. What it will settle for after looking at a number of possible properties is one which roughly satisfies the criteria that have been laid down. To do better than that would involve too much effort and might well be beyond an individual's powers of assessment. Anyway, if a reasonable possibility is found there is often the need to make a decision quickly in case another purchaser steps in, so that further prolonged search for something better may not make tactical sense. The number

	Primary information sources %	Sources used to discover accommodation finally chosen %
Estate agents/flat agencies	13.3	39.6
Newspaper advertisements	20.9	13.4
Friends and relatives	19.8	21.6
By going round district	18.7	4.7
Through local authority	2.9	2.5
At work	4.4	2.5
Business contacts	6.2	9.1
Other, no information	13.8	6.6
	100	100

Table 6 Information sources used to find houses by migrants into four towns in England and Wales (Source: simplified from Johnson, Salt and Wood, 1974)

of houses inspected may depend on the number available, but in the context of a large city it is more likely to be limited by the stamina of the searcher rather than anything else; it may be that as few as three or four houses will be looked at with a serious intention of purchase.

The important conclusion from these observations on search behaviour is that it is unrealistic to interpret house purchase as a completely efficient economic process by which, within the constraints of income, households are fitted into houses which best suit their individual requirements. At the very best it is a matter of households having a constrained knowledge of the geography of housing, with restricted time and energy at their disposal to extend that information base, and possessing a mental map of their surroundings which is shaped by their prejudices, preconceptions and past experiences.

Other constraints on residential choice

In making migration decisions, however, householders are not free agents, since the personal limitations which result from their knowledge and their ability to digest new information are not the only set of constraints which are operating. Obviously, as in any situation where market forces are operating, their financial status restricts the areas in which they will think it worthwhile to search for new accommodation. This factor was implicit in Homer Hoyt's classic sector theory of urban residential structure, in which he noted that residential zones, characterised by particular levels of social status, tended to spread outwards in distinctive sectors of a city. In particular, he observed that areas of high status, with more expensive housing, were most likely to show this feature, presumably because sites adjoining existing high-status areas are very likely to be the most expensive for new building. Later, he was to point out that this process now also operates in a reverse direction in those cities where high-status residential areas are recolonising some of the inner residential areas, again associated with the same general high-status sector. The less well-off may perceive these 'high rent' sectors of the city as attractive, but cannot afford to bid for housing there. This observation is not simply to do with housing status, but also provides a mechanism for explaining the direction of intra-urban moves.

What is perhaps less obvious is that credit-worthiness is probably a more important factor than absolute wealth in the process of bidding for houses, since most people who buy a house require some form of loan to do so. In Britain this is most commonly obtained from a building society. In assessing how much can be lent, the amount of income per annum is important to a building society manager, so that someone with a high annual income but not much money in the bank may be able to bid higher than someone with more capital but with a smaller income. Societies vary in how they calculate the household income, but most now make some allowance for the income which a spouse may bring in. Certain types of occupation are more credit-worthy than others: borrowers with jobs which bring in a regular dependable income with low risk of unemployment are obviously more attractive to a lender than those who may be currently receiving a larger income but have a higher degree of uncertainty associated with their jobs.

Some indication of the selection of different kinds of people by building societies is given in Table 7, which lists the experience of one building society in a sample year. Most borrowers are already owner-occupiers and have thus been shown to be credit-worthy. New mortgages for many of these people allow them to 'trade up' in the housing market and to obtain better properties. Mortgagee are likely to be in their mid-twenties to mid-thirties, and to be in white-collar and skilled manual jobs.

In addition a building society will want to think that the property on which it is advancing a mortgage will maintain its value, in case some misfortune should lead to its having to be sold to repay the loan. As a result certain types of accommodation, like blocks of flats, may be less popular with building societies unless they can be assured that appropriate legal arrangements have been produced to ensure the proper maintenance of the whole property. Similarly, certain areas of the city where residential property values might be expected to fall are also avoided. Some lending agencies have used a process which in the USA is known as 'red-lining', by which certain parts of the city are delimited as being inappropriate for loans. Even if it is not formalised in this way, the reports which surveyors prepare for an individual property in such an area may make purchase of a house there difficult using a building society loan. As a result people for whom such a loan is important may not be able to migrate to particular destinations, and encouragement is given to the building industry to produce rather standardised houses in suburban locations acceptable to building societies and designed for the types of people who are most likely to be deemed credit-worthy by lending agencies.

Other subtle forces operate in the selection of migrants. Estate agents, as they make information available to clients, may push

Tenure	%
Previously owner-occupier	61
Rented privately	7
Rented local authority	9
Living with family/friends	20
Other	3
Total	100

Age%	
Below 26	19
26–35	40
36–45	24
46–55	10
55+	7
Total	100

Employment status	%
Professional/managerial	33
Clerical/junior managerial	17
Skilled manual	27
Semi-skilled manual	8
Retired/widowed/housewife	4
Other	11
Total	100

Table 7 Characteristics of persons granted mortgages in the UK by the Nationwide Building Society, 1987 (Source: Nationwide Building Society)

specific types of property in the direction of particular purchasers. Often they are anxious to make a quick sale and they feel they can achieve this by matching purchaser and property on the basis of what they can guess about the financial status and prejudices of their individual clients. In the USA it has been suggested that racial 'steering' has taken place, by which black purchasers were directed at particular properties in order to maintain exclusively white suburbs. Such a practice is now illegal, but realtors (as estate agents are known in the USA) are products of their own society and share its prejudices, so that an informal selection of purchasers may well continue. Again this is likely to produce distinctive migration streams within a city, particularly if there is a substantial ethnic minority of some kind.

Access to private housing depends on credit-worthiness or on rent-paying ability, although in British cities the amount of property that is available for private renting has been falling rapidly, as potential private landlords see more attractive alternatives for their investments. Many people, however, depend on local authority housing or, increasingly, on accommodation owned by housing associations of various kinds. Access to these houses depends not on wealth, but on meeting certain entrance requirements. To be put on the waiting list for most council housing, for example, it is necessary to have resided in the local area for a period, often a number of years. Then it is necessary to score highly on a points system, designed to assess housing priority and including such indices as lack of alternative accommodation, number of children, state of health, whether homelessness is the result of a slum clearance programme and so on. The officials administering such schemes may have local managerial rules as well, when council tenants seek a transfer because of changing family circumstances or because of changes in the location of work. A tenant with a good record of regular rent paying, having good relations with neighbours, or with the enthusiastic support of a local councillor, may be more favourably treated than a tenant without that kind of recommendation. Such favoured tenants may be offered greater choice in the more desirable housing estates. On the other hand, difficult tenants, perhaps with a record of violence or nuisance, may simply be offered alternative accommodation in so-called 'hard-to-let' estates, with the result that these less desirable houses become even less attractive, ultimately becoming 'impossible-to-let', rather than merely difficult.

As a result it can be said that, for most people, moves within the city are channelled by constraints of this kind and the role of free choice, in which the process of decision making can play an important part, is unimportant. Such a view is too extreme, since even local authority tenants are commonly offered a choice of a number of properties when they are housed or rehoused. Nevertheless the freedom of action that people have is ultimately constrained by the location of available and affordable properties. While individual moves may seem very complex, the end result of the combination of these moves shown in the general pattern of intra-urban migration is relatively simple and underlies the sorting out of the urban residential pattern into socially distinctive neighbourhoods.

3 Internal migration

As indicated in Chapter 1, most modern migration can be classified as internal migration, that is, it takes place within the boundaries of a nation state. Each individual nation provides a distinctive economic and political context for migration of this kind, but there are nevertheless general features associated with different kinds of internal migration. Local movements within cities have already been examined and the concern in this chapter is with longer distance moves, which are important in causing regional demographic, social and economic changes.

In the countries of the modernised world, migration is becoming a more powerful demographic factor in producing changing regional population totals, partly because of declining rates of fertility and also because of related reductions in regional contrasts in natural increase. Labour migration, which forms a significant component of longer distance internal migration, has an important role in matching labour demand with labour supply, and hence in the level of regional economic growth or decline. And because the various types of internal migration involve the selective movement of people of different ages and social classes, they have implications for the social mixture in the areas which lose and gain migrants.

Labour migration

Most long distance migration in developed countries takes place from one urban area to another. In effect local labour markets – towns and cities and their surrounding commuter hinterlands – engage in exchanges in population rather than one-way movements. Almost always there are streams and counterstreams, as suggested originally by Ravenstein. *Net* regional flows of population are generally from less prosperous to more prosperous areas: from the old coalfield and heavy industrial areas in northern England, Scotland and Wales to south-eastern England; or from the Nord-Pas de Calais region of France to the Paris basin, and increasingly to the Mediterranean; or from the northeast of the United States to the 'sunbelt' states of California, the Gulf coast and Florida. At a sub-regional level, however, the gravity principle operates and there is much migration between adjacent local labour market areas, creating regional labour markets within which movement of people occurs. Figure 11 demonstrates that for Great

Britain in 1970–71 the largest flows were between local labour markets. London dominates in terms of numbers moving, but some regional clusters are also obvious, such as the North-west of England, Yorkshire and and central Scotland.

Characteristics of labour migrants

We have already indicated in Chapter 1 that most migrants move short distances. The 1981 Census showed that five million people in Great Britain changed their address during the previous year, 9.6 per cent of the total population. Over half of these moved less than five kilometres and three-quarters less than 20 kilometres; only 13.5 per cent of all movers went over 80 kilometres. Most moves of home are therefore over distances short enough to necessitate no change in job location because they are within commuting range.

Distance moved and reasons for the move are quite closely related. A study of house purchasers in the UK in 1981 showed that three-quarters of all moves of less than five miles were for either housing or life-cycle reasons, and only three per cent were work related. In contrast, three-quarters of moves over 50 miles were for work-related reasons, and only one in five for housing or life-cycle purposes.

Propensity to migrate varies with occupation. Table 8 shows mobility rates in the UK for occupations classified according to a broad ranking by skill level, qualifications and experience needed. In general, rates of mobility decline with skill levels, the main aberration being the 'personal and protective service' category which includes the armed services.

Reasons for labour migration

Socio-economic differences in propensity to move reflect the segmentation of the labour market into occupational categories, some of which have characteristics which encourage mobility while others do not. The traditional economic approach to labour migration stresses its role in the adjustment of supply and demand for labour. If supply exceeds demand in one region, wages there will fall or unemployment will rise; in contrast, in a region with excess demand, no one will be out of work and wages will rise due to the competition among employers for scarce workers. One consequence of this may be that employers will be encouraged to move their activities to a region characterised by a pool of unemployed labour and low wages. This has been the rationale behind the policies adopted by many governments since 1945 to encourage industry to set up in high unemployment areas. Another consequence, though, is for

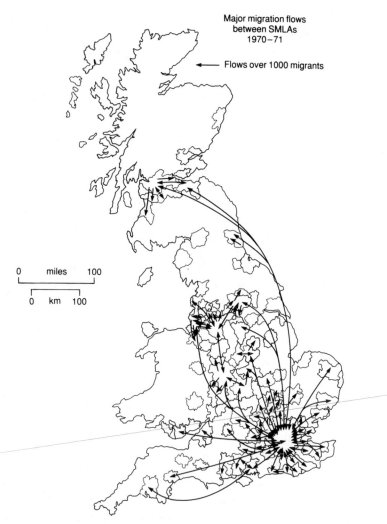

Figure 11 Migration flows of over 1000 migrants between Standard Metropolitan Labour Markets in Great Britain, 1970–71 (Source: simplified from Flowerdew Salt, 1979).

Standard metropolitan labour markets consist of significant clusters of employment and the journey-to-work areas round about them. The map shows the major movements of population in the year before the 1971 census. Not all movers will be labour migrants, since members of their families will also be included in this map and some people who moved between labour markets for non-employment reasons will also be included. However, most of the movement shown here will be associated, directly and indirectly, with labour migration.

Occupational category	Numbers employed (000s)	All moves (%)	Intra regional moves (%)	Inter regional moves (%)
Managers & administrators	3028.1	13.3	9.5	3.8
Professionals	2109.3	13.9	9.1	4.7
Associate professionals and technicians	2262.9	15.0	11.0	4.1
Clerical and secretarial occupations	4354.9	11.6	9.2	2.5
Craft and skilled manual	3943.8	9.9	8.6	1.3
Personal and protective service	1745.1	14.7	10.4	4.3
Sales occupations	1886.2	10.8	8.5	2.3
Plant and machine operatives	2418.7	9.6	8.3	1.3
Other occupations	2504.3	8.5	6.7	1.8
All	24253.3	11.7	9.0	2.7

Highest qualification of men aged 16–64 and women aged 16–59	Numbers with qualification (000s)	All moves (%)	Intra regional moves (%)	Inter regional moves (%)
Higher degree	421.9	18.2	10.0	8.3
Degree	2213.7	20.2	12.4	7.7
BTEC, BEC, TEC Higher	661.0	14.8	9.9	5.0
Teaching/nursing qualification	1248.3	12.9	9.0	3.9
BTEC etc., General, City & Guilds	3475.2	14.2	11.2	3.0
A-level etc.	2110.7	21.0	14.4	6.6
O-level etc.	6185.3	14.1	11.1	3.0
CSE	1797.4	16.3	13.8	2.6
Other professional	2339.2	10.5	7.2	3.3
Other/Not known	581.6	11.1	8.7	2.4
All	21034.3	15.2	11.1	4.1

Table 8 Great Britain: migration by occupational category and highest qualification 1986–7 (Source: 1987 Labour Force Survey)

migration to occur from depressed to prosperous areas as unemployed workers move in search of work. The same theory explains why people who are in work might move from low wage to high wage regions, thus raising their standards of living.

The theory can be extended to take account of occupational specialisation. It would be quite possible, for example, for a stream of migrants in one occupation to move from one region to another while migrants in a different occupation moved in the reverse direction. In reality, though, the labour markets for different occupations are not completely self-contained, and workers in one location may be able to find better jobs locally in another occupational group than undertake a geographical move.

The implications of these arguments are that migration should generally be from regions of low wages and high unemployment to those where the reverse holds, and that it should be in those occupations where the greatest interregional differences in pay exist. It is also to be expected, however, that ease of entry to an occupation will affect migration. For those jobs requiring specialist qualifications or long periods of training, regional imbalances are more likely to be cured by migrants. In contrast, occupations requiring little by way of qualifications or training may be filled through occupational rather than geographical mobility. It follows, then, that interregional migration is more likely to involve skilled or professional workers than those who are unskilled.

Reasons for migration are not only economic, and there are sociological arguments which suggest that not everyone will be equally inclined to migrate. For many people factors other than employment are more important, like attachment to family and community, and it is known that these vary between classes and occupations. The act of migration will break a wide variety of ties, not all of which will be the same for all members of a household. The importance of these ties often depends on previous migration experience; those who have moved frequently will have put down shallower roots than those who have lived all their lives in the same place, and normally will find another move easier than someone contemplating their first change of location. Indeed, for some people staying put may be a better solution than leaving, despite what at first might seem common sense. Unemployed people, for example, may feel they can maximise their happiness locally, in the area, house and community they know, rather than undertake the expense of moving to where jobs are available but where there is, perhaps, uncertainty about how long those jobs might last and how easy it would be to establish an appealing social life.

Occupational differences in migration propensity

All sectors of the population are engaged in labour migration, but it is the higher socio-economic groups – professionals, managers and other white-collar workers – who are more likely to move. Why should this be so? For these people labour migration is often associated with career development. Promotion, experience and higher salaries are frequently achieved through a change of job, so mobility can become an essential element in life style. Such workers are also more likely to have the financial resources to enable them to migrate. Employers, too, may seek to fill vacancies requiring specialist skills and experience from over a wide area. The information channels they use to find workers, such as national newspapers and trade and professional journals, have a wide geographical circulation and are likely to be seen by potential employees in other towns and cities. In contrast, employers seeking low-skilled workers tend to look only locally, and use geographically restricted channels of information like local newspapers and Jobcentres, so these opportunities are not easily found out about by workers elsewhere who might want to move.

These advantages for more highly skilled workers are compounded by the practice of many large employers of paying the removal and other expenses of the more specialist workers they recruit. Large employers with more than one site are also likely to transfer their managerial and professional staff from one part of the country to another, usually as part of career development. Not only does this practice considerably increase the amount of labour migration that goes on, but those who move usually have all their expenses paid. Furthermore, relocation agencies exist to make the transfer as smooth as possible. They help these migrants sell their houses and buy new ones, and will arrange bridging finance if necessary. They provide a 'magic carpet' for the migrant, all costs being paid by the employer.

For low-skilled and especially unemployed people the situation is very different. We have already seen that economic theories of migration would seem to suggest that the unemployed move in search of jobs elsewhere, but the evidence in many developed countries is that the unemployed are less likely to move to another area than those with jobs. There are a number of reasons for this. Often they lack the financial resources to move; and they may also have difficulty finding out about jobs elsewhere. Housing problems loom large: if they own their own homes they may have difficulty selling, or there may be a large price difference between what they can get for their house, especially if it is in a depressed area, and what a similar house would cost in a prosperous area. If they currently rent their homes, perhaps from the local authority, there are often problems in even getting on the waiting list in a new area. Finally, there is evidence that unemployed people often become enmeshed in a social web, with others in the same circumstances, and with a strong sense of community and self-help. In these cases it makes more sense for the unemployed to stay put, capitalising on the social advantages they have, rather than move to another area where they may know few people, and are uncertain about job prospects.

Government policies on labour migration

Government interest in migration tends to be keen because of its effects on both origin and destination areas. Local authority finance is affected by changes in numbers of local taxpayers. Service provision may need to adjust to variable numbers of children or elderly; one of the key determinants in forecasting primary school rolls, for example, is an estimate of the level of net migration of under fives. Land-use planning policies are influenced by migration. The allocation of investment in housing needs to be sensitive to migration flows, since new pressures on land allocation may be created by migration growth areas, such as the arc to the west and north of London or to the west of Paris. In the areas of net out-migration there may be considerable capital in the form of houses, schools and transport infrastructure that is underused. It is also politically difficult for a government to preside over a decline in local and regional population.

For all these reasons most governments adopt regional policies which are designed to maintain existing population levels, normally through policies of helping the work to go to the workers rather than vice versa. Few have adopted policies directly intended to encourage people to move. A survey across western Europe in the late 1970s found most governments wanted to reduce the level of migration, and were actively engaged in trying to bring this about through planning policies designed to restrict the amount of building land in growth areas, while at the same time giving investment grants and other incentives to help hold people in those areas that were declining.

Government policies towards migration thus fall into three main categories: to preserve regions from population decline, usually by a regional policy designed to channel investment into areas of economic difficulty (moving work to the workers); to solve the unemployment problem by helping some people to move (moving workers to the work); and to improve urban living conditions by relocating urban populations into new towns.

(a) Work to the workers
Many governments have sought to create employment and prosperity in regions of decline. Implicit in such policies has been the

restriction of out-migration from these regions because of the important economic and social effects that would be caused, especially as it would be the most active and skilled who were likely to leave first. Complementary to this has been the desire to relieve the pressures on land, housing and other social resources in the more prosperous areas.

These policies depend for their success upon general economic prosperity and the consequent existence of 'mobile employment' capable of being relocated in areas that are perhaps not naturally favoured. In France during the 1960s and 1970s a policy was adopted of using central government finance to develop its *metropoles d'équilibres*. These are provincial cities like Nantes and Lille, designed to anchor investment and population in provincial France and to attract people and jobs that would otherwise move to the Ile de France region. In the UK regional policy was at its most successful in the 1960s, and between 1963 and 1974 about 250,000 extra jobs were created in the assisted areas. Of course, it is not possible to be sure about the migration consequences of this increase, but one estimate is that without it the rate of out-migration from the less prosperous areas would have been twice as high as it was.

(b) Workers to the work

A number of governments have tried to deal with the lack of geographical mobility among the unemployed by the introduction of policy measures designed to help them move.

One example of a government scheme designed to help the unemployed move to regions where jobs were available was the Employment Transfer Scheme in the UK. Under the scheme the government paid part of the removal costs of unemployed people who obtained jobs in other parts of the country. Begun in 1928 to help unemployed miners move from declining coalfields, it became a more general scheme after the Second World War, though it rarely moved more than a few thousand a year. During the 1970s it reached a postwar height, moving 26,000 workers plus their families in one year. It was abolished in 1986.

Such policies have been vigorously debated. Some people argue that encouraging people to move unleashes cumulative forces of decline in the origin regions. It is suggested that this leads to the underuse of social capital and infrastructure, to the disintegration of communities, and to the loss of political power. However, there is almost no evidence that these consequences do ensue. This is largely because most government migration schemes involve quite small numbers of people and their effect cannot easily be detected.

(c) New towns

One type of government migration policy that is common to a number of countries is that associated with the development of new towns. The best known examples are those in Britain, but the principle has been widely adopted. The idea of new towns is to create entirely new communities, either on 'greenfield' sites or based around small existing settlements. By definition most of the population of these new settlements is migratory.

There are basically two types of new town. The first type is designed to take overspill population from major cities, and to divert flows currently going to them. Examples of this type of new town include Basildon and Stevenage around London, Runcorn near Liverpool and Marne La Vallée to the east of Paris. The second type is designed to act as a focus for regional development. Examples include Cwmbran in South Wales and Washington in north-east England. In addition to the new towns the UK government has developed a series of expanded towns – that is, existing communities upon which major new urban development has been grafted. The new towns programme began in the late 1940s and by 1973 28 new or expanded towns housed 1.7 million people and had provided over 200,000 dwellings.

From the outset the aim of the British new towns was to provide socially balanced communities, and by and large they have been successful. The socio-economic structure of migrants to the ring of new towns around London, for example, is similar to that of Greater London residents as a whole. More recent UK new towns, like Milton Keynes, have also built up reasonably balanced communities, having successfully attracted in a wide variety of industries and services and built a range of types of housing.

Migration between rural and urban areas

In the advanced economies of the world movement is commonly from one urban area to another, but in the nineteenth century movement from rural to urban areas was of great importance in facilitating the growth of cities. In the early decades of the twentieth century, although rural-urban migration was much less important for urban growth, it continued the process of rural depopulation at a high percentage level. In more recent decades, however, rural-urban migration has been quantitatively much less important in the developed world, as distinctively rural employment has fallen close to an irreducible minimum. Indeed, in recent decades there is evidence that in some rural areas population has been increasing again, and the term *counterurbanisation* has been applied to this process, although there are problems in definition here which must be returned to later. In the developing world, in contrast, rural-urban migration is still of growing significance, with important implications in these regions for other geographical phenomena like, for example, the growth of squatter settlements.

Rural depopulation and migration

Rural-urban migration must be set in the context of the variety of possible demographic situations which can exist in rural areas. In particular it should be noted that rural depopulation is not an inescapable result of rural-urban migration, since a reduction in the population of a rural area can be caused by a variety of situations. For example, death rates may be higher than birth rates, giving natural decrease which would result in rural depopulation unless natural loss was off-set by in-migration. Another possibility is that net outward movement may be higher than natural increase, giving a fall in total population. Or again, rural depopulation would be enhanced if net out-migration were combined with natural decrease. In other words the effect of out-migration on the total population depends upon the general demographic situation in the rural area concerned (Figure 12).

Out-migration itself has a direct influence on other demographic characteristics by selectively removing young adults in the fertile age groups, thus reducing the overall fertility of the remaining population, and hence increasing the impact of emigration on population totals. Although rural depopulation is the usual result of rural-urban migration, it is not an inevitable product of the process, as current evidence from many parts of the developing world indicates. Here natural increase often more than off-sets the loss of population by rural-urban migration, so that rural population increase continues in spite of net outward movement of population.

In the twentieth-century developed world, on the other hand, rural-urban migration has taken place in the context of sharply falling rates of natural increase in rural areas and has very frequently produced falls in total population numbers. Rural depopulation of this kind has been largely associated with the decline of agricultural employment, although the contraction of rural craft industries in the face of competition from urban factories, and the increased provision of rural services from towns and cities, have also contributed to the process. In some cases rural workers have been able to switch to urban employment, but at the same time have retained their existing

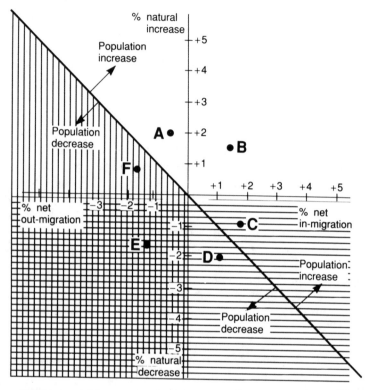

Figure 12 Demographic contexts of population change

Population change can be produced by a variety of demographic combinations. Six hypothetical areas are located on the graph above. Areas D, E and F are all experiencing population decline: in D net in-migration is more than off-set by natural decrease; in E out-migration and natural decrease combine to produce decline; in F out-migration more than off-sets natural increase. Similarly areas A, B and C are all experiencing population growth, but again with different combinations of migration and natural change.

rural residences. This occurs in locations where members of farm families and other rural residents are able to commute to work in nearby towns. In more remote areas such possibilities are much more limited, and it is here that rural-urban migration appears to have had most impact, since its effects in causing rural depopulation are most clearly seen because there is little or no off-setting in-migration. However, rural-urban migration is likely to have occurred in most rural areas, although close to major cities it is masked by the movement in of formerly urban-based commuters and retired people.

In the Western world, although the percentage decline in rural population in some limited areas may still be considerable, the scope for large absolute movements of people from rural to urban areas has now largely been exhausted. Elsewhere urban growth is still proceeding at very high rates and, although natural increase is often important in the growth of urban populations, the attraction of in-migration from rural areas remains very important. For example, in Third World cities as diverse as Seoul, Lagos and Djakarta migrants represented more than 50 per cent of the total population increase in recent decades. As a secondary effect, this in-migration introduces into the urban population young adults who have higher levels of fertility than the population as a whole, hence increasing rates of natural increase in the growing cities.

Not all these migrants come direct from the countryside to large cities. Small towns often provide a link in the movement of population from rural area to large cities, since migration is often through smaller urban settlements where migrants from rural areas may fail to find long-term employment, but where they make their first adjustments to urban life before facing the greater challenge of living in a major metropolis. Such a process is known as *step-wise migration* (Figure 13).

One result of rural-urban migration is the presence of a large number of poor people in the larger cities of the developing world, who live in shanty or squatter settlements, which are often located on the periphery of the city. It might be better to call these shanties 'uncontrolled' rather than 'squatter' settlements, since their particular legal status is frequently a matter of some doubt. So, too, is their role in urban society. At first sight they may seem like groups of squalid homes inhabited by the dregs of society. The apparently obvious interpretation is that the migrants consist of the poorest rural dwellers who have been driven out by the extreme poverty in their home areas to pick up a marginally better living in the informal sector of the labour market of a large city; but studies in Latin America have suggested that, in parts of this region at least, this is not always the case. Often the migrants turn out to be better educated and more skilled than many in the rural area from which they came. In other words they may consist of the more enterprising among rural dwellers.

Further complications to generally-held views are provided by research which shows that not all the inhabitants of the shanty towns come direct from the countryside. Many have occupied rented

Forms of step-wise migration

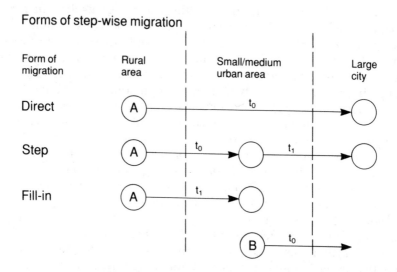

Figure 13 Forms of step-wise migration

Some forms of step-wise migration are depicted in this diagram. In the first case migrant A moves directly from a rural area to a large city. In the second case the migration occurs in steps, first to a small or medium-sized urban area during time t_0, then subsequently (time t_1) to the large city. Fill-in migration happens when migrant A's move follows the creation of a vacancy by B's move to the large city. In practice all three forms may occur simultaneously. Although developed in the context of third-world rural to urban movement, the forms of movement can be adapted to most inter-regional and even international migrations.

accommodation in inner-city slums before moving to shanty settlements and their shanty homes represent the first step in acquiring property of their own. With the passage of time some shanty areas have been greatly improved by their inhabitants, as they have become better established in the urban economy. In fact, it is difficult to generalise about these matters since what may be true in one region does not apply in others, and squatter settlements exhibit a wide range of social conditions. In particular, the desperate situation in some Asian settlements may not offer the opportunities for upward economic mobility which seem possible in some parts of Latin America. What can be said is that these uncontrolled settlements are a morphological expression of the pressure on housing for lower paid workers produced by the rapid growth of cities, to which rural-urban migration makes a most important contribution.

Counterurbanisation

By way of contrast, in recent decades the highly developed parts of the world have experienced what at first sight appears to be a reverse trend to rural-urban migration. This is the process of counterurbanisation by which large cities seem to be losing population by net migration to non-metropolitan areas. The term 'counterurbanisation' was first used to describe some elements of population change in the USA in the early 1970s, but the same phenomenon has also been recorded in Britain and in Western Europe.

In fact migration into some rural areas of a size sufficient to produce a rise in the recorded population is of much longer standing. In Britain, for example, some accessible and scenically attractive rural areas showed an increase in population in the 1920s and 1930s as a result of the in-migration of retired people. Counterurbanisation, however, is a more widespread feature and is also associated with a stagnation or actual fall in population growth in the larger metropolitan areas, which is a more recent occurrence.

In popular thought counterurbanisation is associated with the idea that some sort of rural renaissance has been taking place. Images inevitably spring to mind of people returning to the land to live on small holdings or supporting themselves by rural crafts. Such people exist, but their numbers are small; and a variety of other factors, often unrelated to one another, are involved in producing this condition.

One prosaic element is simply the problem of interpreting 'rural' and 'urban' conditions from census information. People who have taken advantage of improved personal mobility to move to locations beyond the limits of formal suburbs will often be classified as rural, although functionally they are still strongly connected with a central city which provides them with employment and more specialised services. At a broader scale, however, it appears that much of the movement that makes up counterurbanisation is taking place between larger cities and smaller urban settlements, rather than to the open countryside. For example in the United States a large element in the process of counterurbanisation consists of a movement to the smaller cities and towns of the country's southern and western states, the so-called 'Sunbelt'.

In addition to low density residential areas within the zone of influence of large cities but not directly linked to them in census returns, there are other factors which it is necessary to invoke to explain the phenomenon. For example, retirement moves to environmentally attractive regions continue at an increased level in those countries where older people are affluent enough to consider such a move and find it socially appealing. The growing importance of second homes, which are purchased with holidays in mind, must also be part of the story, although for that to show up in the census statistics the use of the second home for a vacation must also coincide with the date on which the population census is taken.

But, at a broader national scale, counterurbanisation is more often than not the product of the more rapid growth of employment in the smaller towns and cities, in comparison with the largest settlements, rather than any genuine revival of the true countryside. In the advanced economies it is now technically possible for an increasing number of jobs to be free of any particular urban settlement, aided in part by the development of telecommunications. As a result employers are freer to seek cheaper, less unionised labour which may be available in smaller, more remote settlements, in order to reduce their production costs in a competitive world. Similarly, skilled professional workers increasingly prefer the social and physical environments provided by smaller settlements, and employers in high-tech industries may find it easier to recruit these workers in settlements noted for their pleasant living conditions, rather than for their industrial histories.

Some recent evidence from the United States and for Great Britain suggests that many large cities have now checked their rates of decline or, indeed, have reversed the process. As a result, at present it remains a matter for debate whether counterurbanisation is a passing phenomenon or whether it will eventually turn out to be a more fundamental social and economic trend.

Retirement migration

Although it is probable that the migration of population following retirement forms a constituent part of counterurbanisation, it is a process that has been going on for many decades among the more affluent sections of western society. The growth in the importance of retirement movement is, however, relatively recent. It is also a movement which in total is much more often than not from one urban centre to another, rather than to rural areas, strictly defined.

However, there is some evidence of a distinct sequence of destinations as retirement migration has developed. At an early stage of rapid urbanisation many retirement migrants tend to return to rural areas from which they had migrated earlier in life. This stage is still important, for example, in France. At a later stage, restricted areas which are perceived as having an attractive environment are sought out, like parts of Florida in the United States. Finally, the destinations of retirement migrants become more dispersed, because of increased numbers and because the original retirement towns have become more expensive and less attractive. For example, central Bournemouth in southern England is no longer highly rated as a retirement destination, although earlier it was fashionable for that purpose.

Retirement migration is partly a reflection of increasing affluence, as more people find they have the resources to live independently after retirement. It is also a movement that is encouraged by the fact that an increasing number of people, particularly professional workers, move quite frequently during their working lives, so that they do not put down such deep roots in a particular community. In turn the children of these workers are themselves likely to move away from their home areas when they enter employment, so that the family ties of an increasing number of parents are not restricted to a particular locality. In these circumstances older people feel freer to seek retirement homes in areas which appear environmentally attractive to them. Certainly this is a form of migration which cannot be interpreted in terms of regional variations in employment opportunities, since it is motivated by factors other than job-seeking.

As has already been seen there is a strong tendency for older people to change their residences at the time of their retirement, although this often may simply involve a local intra-urban move, motivated by the need to find a more easily managed and, perhaps, cheaper home. Retirement migration, however, implies a move to another locality. The distance of the journey to work is no longer important and as a result the household has greater freedom in choosing its location. Environmental considerations, including the availability of suitable housing for older people, take on much greater significance. So, too, do accessibility to grown-up children and grand-children.

Retirement migration sometimes involves long distances. In the United States, for example, states like Arizona and Florida have been attracting retirement migration from areas as far away as the North-East United States. In Britain the distance involved is necessarily much less: areas along the south coast have been particularly attractive, but the phenomenon is common in other coastal areas like those of north-west England and East Anglia (Fig. 14). In the United States it has been suggested that the lower heating bills of the Sun-

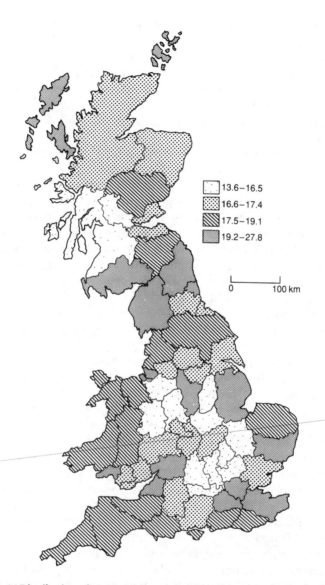

☐	13.6−16.5
▨	16.6−17.4
▧	17.5−19.1
■	19.2−27.8

0   100 km

Figure 14 Distribution of pensionable population in Great Britain 1981 (After: Warnes and Law, 1984)

The pensionable population of Britain consists of men over 65 and women over 60. The map is based on counties in England and Wales, and on regional council areas in Scotland and shows the pensionable population as a percentage of the total population.

belt are appealing to these migrants, but often much less easily quantifiable elements are involved in the decision. One important consideration, for example, appears to be the desire to be associated with a seemingly more traditional life style, thought to be found in a small town in contrast to the impersonality of a large city, although a romantic perception of some lost rural idyll rather than careful objective appraisal must play an important part in that assessment.

The movement is dominated by the better-off, partly because they are more aware of opportunities over a wider area; and as a result the destination of the movement is likely to be influenced by past experience. One theory is that the experience of summer holidays earlier in life produces happy memories of locations which seem attractive destinations – hence, for example, the attraction of coastal resorts in Britain. However, an important contributory factor is also that housing developers are increasingly providing suitable accommodation in such locations, designed for sale to the more affluent elderly, hence reinforcing the importance of these destinations.

It is difficult to establish whether or not retirement migration benefits the small towns where it occurs. Some consider it socially undesirable for the population of a town to be increasingly dominated by older people, although in fairness it is hard to argue that facilities aimed at younger people have been worsened by their presence, since they usually represent an addition to the existing population rather than a replacement. By maintaining or increasing the total urban population, well-off retired people help to maintain and expand shopping facilities. The more active among them often make a real contribution to local community activities, as they have time to spare and may well bring the experience derived from highly responsible working lives. In due course, however, their presence places an increased strain on medical services, since special hospital and other facilities are needed as they grow older. Similarly, the housing first chosen for retirement may turn out to be less satisfactory with the passage of time, producing a requirement for older people's bungalows and other forms of sheltered housing.

However, it can be argued that these needs would occur wherever older people live. What really is involved is the grouping of these special facilities in particular places rather than their even spread across the nation, since the total demand must stay the same. There may be real advantages in the concentration of demand for services designed to help elderly people, provided that the costs of a national responsibility do not fall unfairly on local tax-payers.

4 International migration

The colonisation of the globe is a story of human migration to settle new lands. From the end of the medieval period Europeans ventured overseas to the New World, a tide rising to its peak in the nineteenth century. Australasia, and especially the Americas, provided lands of opportunity for Europeans, the small indigenous populations being able to put up little resistance to the incoming settlers. Tropical areas were generally shunned by those used to temperate climates unless the hot environment with its diseases could be tempered by altitude. Asia was never a major area of European immigration, though Chinese peoples spread widely throughout the south and east of the continent. Not all movement was voluntary. An estimated 50 million people were carried off in the slave trade, and after its abolition indentured labourers were used in European-owned plantations in the Far East and Australasia.

Today, international migration adopts a variety of guises. Three basic types of movement may be recognised: *permanent settlement, temporary labour* and *asylum-seeking*. Migrants may become permanent immigrants for a variety of reasons. They may move within some form of settler scheme, normally under government auspices. Others may come initially as temporary immigrants but subsequently be allowed to register as long-stay immigrants, granting a more or less permanent right of abode. Some obtain naturalisation, usually after residing in the destination country for several years, giving them full citizenship rights in their new country. Family reunion is another avenue to permanent settlement. When one member of a family has established a right of permanent abode, he or she may be allowed to bring in close kin who are also entitled to that status.

Temporary labour migration is anything but homogeneous. It may be seasonal, particularly amongst agricultural workers, or on longer term contracts. The form of contract may vary, from a set calendar period to the completion of a project, like building a dam or a power station. The types of labour involved range widely, from unskilled workers, doing the jobs which the indigenous labour force does not want, to highly skilled people who have specialist skills in short supply. Both men and women are temporary labour migrants; in the past the former have been more likely to move, especially as most work has been in manufacturing, mining or construction. Increasingly now, though, such movement is of women going to work as domestic servants, or in other service industries.

There are also some types of movement that are more ephemeral but which have implications for international migration. Migration of students from poorer to richer countries can lead ultimately to transfers of technology when they return; often, though, they stay on, leading to a brain drain. Businessmen and tourists constitute the bulk of those who move internationally. Mostly these are not classed as migrants, although in some cases the duration of stay may extend into weeks and months.

Role of the state

What all these types of migration have in common is that they involve moves across international borders. Consequently movement occurs from the jurisdiction of one state to another. Some countries allow relatively free movement across their borders while others are more restrictive: hence we sometimes talk about open and closed borders to population movement. In the nineteenth century most borders were open but during the present century states have gradually exercised greater control over entry and borders are now generally more closed. Thus, although we may recognise migrations between states that have similarities with forms of internal migration – rural-urban moves, moves in search of work, family or individual moves, those that are forced or voluntary – we must recognise the paramountcy of state control over who should cross national boundaries.

Legacies of past moves, which may not have been international at the time, often create problems of political and ethnic minorities in today's nation states. Asians brought to East and South Africa by the British now form distinctive minority groups there. The presence of such adventitious populations can lead to delicate political balances between races, as in Malaysia where Malays, Indians and Chinese are the main groups, but which can easily be broken as was the case in Fiji in 1987. In Northern Ireland past migrations from Britain underlie the present troubles. In much of Africa the imposition of colonial borders often had little regard for traditional ethnic and cultural links. After independence, movement continued as of old, crossing the new international boundaries usually without any form of political control.

All modern states have developed policies towards immigration, rather fewer towards emigration, at least of their own citizens. The role of the state is dominant in controlling movement between countries and in granting rights of abode. We can recognise five principal roles for the state in international migration.

First, the state controls entry through laws and regulations. It does this in two ways. Through its nationality and citizenship laws it decides who may freely come into the country without let or hindrance, i.e. it specifies the criteria for citizenship. By virtue of its immigration rules it decides which non-citizens may enter and for how long and under what conditions. In the UK the government controls immigration through two major pieces of legislation, the Immigration Act (1971) and the British Nationality Act (1981). The first contains the rules which are operated by immigration officers at ports and airports and which tell them who is permitted to enter. The second defines those who are entitled to British citizenship and who are free to come and go as they please.

Second, some states choose to restrict exit of their citizens. Until 1989 this was common practice among the communist states of eastern Europe and the USSR. The Berlin Wall, for example, was built in 1961 to prevent East Germans moving to the West. With the breakdown of the Soviet Empire, those countries now preventing their citizens leaving freely are, with the major exception of the People's Republic of China, dictatorships.

Third, some states engage with others in allowing free circulation of their citizens. Perhaps the best known formal systems are those of the EC and Nordic countries, but relatively free flows also exist in theory in the West African economic region (ECOWAS) and, in practice, between Canada and the USA. Within the European Community and within the Nordic group of countries (Sweden, Finland, Norway and Denmark) fellow citizens are allowed to travel freely to seek and take work and to settle without being subjected to immigration control at national borders. This has resulted in substantial exchanges of population, though no one can be sure how many people move because one consequence of lack of control is that few statistics are kept on cross-border movement of community citizens.

Fourth, the state frequently sets up an administrative apparatus to control flows. Some states, France and Canada for example, have special ministries to deal with matters of immigration and emigration. In order to recruit workers it has been the practice to set up official recruiting offices in origin countries, as West Germany did in Yugoslavia and Turkey in the 1960s and early 1970s. Countries from which workers emigrate may also seek to formalise the process of emigration: for example, the Philippines government has set up the Philippines Overseas Employment Administration to coordinate recruitment of Filipinos for work overseas, mainly in the Arabian Gulf, and to look after their citizens working abroad by monitoring their living and working conditions.

Finally, through the institution of cross-border checks, censuses and administrative procedures, governments are the main source of data on international migration. However, the extent of coverage and accuracy of the data vary enormously. Emigration data are almost always poorer than immigration data because most countries control (and therefore count) those coming in more than those leaving. Numbers of illegal migrants are the most problematical, since by definition they escape official counting systems.

The geography of international migration

Figure 15 attempts to summarise the main international migration flows c.1990. It includes the main settlement and labour flows, but not those of refugees. Such a map must be regarded as a guide rather than a definitive statement, since there is no comprehensive source of data.

The world map of international migration shows a series of distinct spatial systems consisting of regional groupings of countries between which flows occur. Superimposed upon these are flows which are intercontinental in character and which include moves between former colonies and their mother countries and also the temporary migrations of highly skilled businessmen and professionals. At any one time these systems are in different stages of evolution and their exact form reflects a complexity of economic, political, social and geographical situations.

Within each geographical system, flows link some countries but not others and, within countries, particular regions are especially associated with emigration or immigration. Indeed it is common for flows to develop and be maintained between pairs of regions, for example between Senegal Valley and parts of Paris, and between specific villages in southern Italy and those parts of Bedfordshire where Italians came to work in the brick industry. These links have come about because of the chain effects of migration. Once a channel of migration has become established, those who have moved report back, encouraging others to follow them. The migrants also provide a point of contact for their family and friends, perhaps providing them with somewhere to stay upon arrival and helping them to find a job. In this way international migration may be regarded as an extended form of regional migration. Two of the main international migration systems are described briefly below.

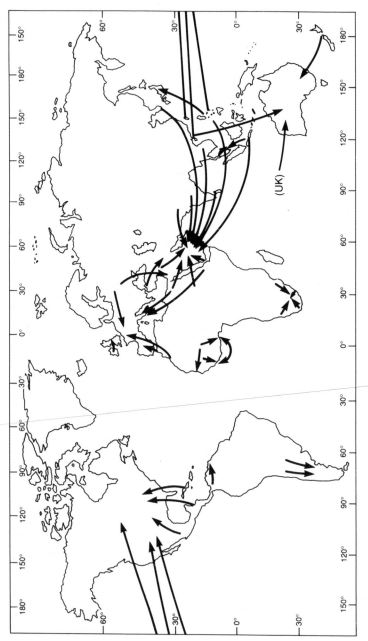

Figure 15 **Principal migration flows, c. 1990 (excluding refugees)**

(UK)

Western Europe

Throughout much of the twentieth century the region has been characterised by large scale international movements of population. The Second World War and its aftermath is reckoned to have involved 25 million moves. During the 1940s and 1950s Germans from the eastern lands resettled in the Federal Republic; Italians came to work in France, Switzerland and the UK; Finns moved into Sweden to work. The 1960s and early 1970s saw millions of Mediterraneaners moving north to work, and the European labour market extended to former French lands in West Africa. Cheap labour became a major factor in the postwar economic growth of the region. Exchanges of population between the industrial countries, mainly involving skilled workers and their families, grew in importance.

After 1973 economic recession stemmed further large scale movement of workers from the Mediterranean lands. However, workers who had previously moved north did not return home but instead chose to bring their families to join them. What had begun as temporary labour migration became a permanent movement with the settlement of minority groups of Iberians, Italians, Turks, Yugoslavs and North Africans in the northern industrial states. Table 9 shows the size of the immigrant population in selected European countries, and where they have come from.

During the 1980s the region experienced two new types of flows. First, numbers of refugees increased sharply, initially from Third World origins, but in the late 1980s there were flows from Eastern Europe. Second, Italy and Spain, both former labour exporting countries, began themselves to receive large numbers of African immigrant workers as their economies improved and demanded workers willing to do low-paid, unskilled jobs. By 1990 fears of mass immigration from the East and the South, a steep rise in asylum-seeking, and the growth of anti-immigrant feeling in some states, forced international migration to the top of the European policy agenda.

The Middle East

Vast increases in oil revenues in the 1970s and small local populations resulted in the Gulf states importing large numbers of workers, mainly unskilled, to build houses, refineries, hospitals, universities, roads, airports and the like. Most of these workers were from the Indian subcontinent though many also came from countries in south-east Asia, like South Korea and the Philippines. By the middle 1980s there were an estimated three to four million foreign workers in the region (Table 10). They were employed on a strict contractual basis and were

	Belgium 1988	France 1985	Germany 1988	Netherlands 1988	Norway 1988	Sweden 1988	Switzerland 1988
Austria	..	..	155.1	3.0	0.5	2.8	28.6
Finland	..	..	9.0	..	3.6	127.9	1.5
Greece	20.6	..	274.8	4.3	0.3	7.1	8.4
Italy	241.0	277.1	508.7	16.0	0.8	3.9	382.3
Portugal	13.5	751.3	71.1	8.0	0.4	1.5	57.6
Spain	52.5	267.9	126.4	17.4	0.9	2.8	114.0
Turkey	79.5	146.1	1523.7	176.5	4.9	23.0	56.8
Yugoslavia	5.4	..	579.1	12.1	3.0	38.9	100.7
Algeria	10.6	820.9	5.1	0.7	..	..	2.0
Morocco	135.5	516.4	52.1	139.2	1.9	1.1	1.8
Tunisia	6.2	202.6	21.6	2.7	..	..	2.5
Other countries	304.0	769.9	1162.4	243.8	119.6	212.0	250.3
Total	868.8	3752.2	4489.1	623.7	135.9	421.0	1006.5
As % of total population	8.8	6.8	7.3	4.2	3.2	5.0	15.3

Table 9 Foreign population in selected OECD countries (000s) (Source: OECD, 1990)

not encouraged to bring their families. However, recent indications are that some workers have not returned home at the end of their contracts and that family members have followed them to the Gulf.

In addition to the great mass of unskilled labourers engaged in building projects, the Gulf oil industry has traditionally employed highly skilled expatriates, and these have been joined by other professionals such as engineers, doctors and nurses and teachers from Europe, North America, Japan and increasingly from the newly industrialising countries such as South Korea, Taiwan and China. A growing feature is the importance of female domestic servants, especially from Sri Lanka and the Philippines.

Permanent international migration

Although the days of 'empty' lands waiting to be settled are now over, there are still many people who move with the intention of settling permanently in another country. For many, migration does indeed become permanent; others stay for a while and then decide to return. Some of those who return do so quite quickly. Others may be 30 or 40 years abroad, returning to their birthplaces to retire: many Italians who went to the USA earlier this century have done this. Often temporary migrants stay away much longer than they originally intended, in effect becoming settlers in their new country. Many Turks and Yugoslavs, for example, who were temporary migrants to West Germany in the 1960s, subsequently stayed on.

During the nineteenth and early twentieth centuries migration for settlement in lands of opportunity was the main type of long distance movement. In the century from 1830 the USA absorbed 24 million migrants; it still takes 600,000 permanent immigrants a year today, making it the single biggest destination. Today most countries in the world accept some new settlers but few actively encourage new settlement immigration. Those that do usually operate a quota system, allowing in a set number each year. Only the USA, Canada, Australia, New Zealand and Israel may be said actively to encourage new settlement, that is, they convey full citizenship rights upon acceptance for entry. Since the Second World War Australia has been regarded as the epitome of immigrant countries for Britons seeking a new life abroad. After 1945 the Australian government, anxious to attract immigrants from the UK, established an assisted passage scheme which operated until 1973. Would-be settlers had their fares to Australia paid, except for a nominal £10, which gave them the description of 'ten pound migrants'.

	Bahrain	Kuwait	Oman	Qatar	Saudi Arabia	UAE	Total
Nationality Group:							
Arab	7,600	252,900	20,900	16,400	1,154,200	95,500	1,547,500
South Asian	70,900	242,700	280,800	46,200	1,126,300	447,700	2,214,600
South-east Asian	10,700	31,200	4,600	4,000	968,400	25,000	1,043,900
Other	7,700	17,100	7,800	4,100	273,800	30,300	340,800
Total	96,900	543,900	314,100	70,700	3,522,700	598,500	5,146,800

%	Bahrain	Kuwait	Oman	Qatar	Saudi Arabia	UAE	Total
Nationality Group:							
Arab	7.8	46.5	6.6	23.2	32.8	16.0	30.1
South Asian	73.2	44.6	89.4	65.3	32.0	74.8	43.0
South-east Asian	11.1	5.7	1.5	5.7	27.4	4.2	20.3
Other	7.9	3.2	2.5	5.8	7.8	5.0	6.6
Total	100.0	100.0	100.0	100.0	100.0	100.0	100.0

Table 10 1985 Non-national workforce stocks by nationality group and country of employment (Source: Birks, Seccombe & Sinclair, 1988)

In recent years even these countries have been more reluctant to encourage new settlers, accepting only immigrants whose skills are needed by their economies. There is evidence now, though, that some countries may be reconsidering their settlement policies for demographic reasons. Canada, concerned at falling birth rates, announced in 1987 that it was to increase its immigration quota by ten per cent per annum. However, the settlement countries are not likely to provide much of a safety valve for the world's overpopulated countries. Together their annual intake is a tiny fraction of the net increase in the world's population, and the time is long past when masses of poor people could look forward to starting a new life overseas.

Much settlement migration today results from the end of colonial rule. When independence came, the citizens of former dependent territories were often given the opportunity of retaining the citizenship of the colonial power or opting for that of the new state. Many of them moved to the mother country at the time of independence; others stayed but retained the right to migrate later. This explains the migration links between the UK and the Indian subcontinent, France and North and West Africa, the Netherlands and the Antilles and Surinam. Figures for the UK show that 25 per cent of those granted right to settle in 1988 came from the subcontinent. This is, in fact, a relatively recent movement, beginning in earnest in the 1960s, and before that the main immigration for settlement was from the West Indies.

Temporary labour migration

Most international migration today is temporary labour movement and is a response to differences between countries in standards of living. Those involved go to live and work in another country, usually in an attempt to raise their standard of living by earning more than if they stayed at home. They have been described as 'target' workers, the target being a sum of money to be gained over a period of a year or two. For some the target is soon found to be unattainable in the time originally allotted, so the expected period abroad is lengthened. Others change their targets, especially upon exposure to a more consumer-based society than the one they have left, and feel that with a longer period abroad they can be even better off. In both of these cases what was originally intended as a short period away may become more permanent.

Mostly it is young and single adults, especially men, who move. Reasons for labour migration may be sought at both origins and destinations, but are closely bound up with economic differences. Temporary movement can evolve into either return migration or permanent settlement. Many who return home re-emigrate subsequently. Those who stay in the new country often bring their families over to join them. The pattern in western Europe in the last 30 years has been for an initial flow of workers to be transformed into a flow of dependants as spouses and children have followed.

Most people involved in labour migrations have been relatively unskilled, but an important element in recent years has been the movement of highly skilled people in what are termed 'brain drains', perhaps more correctly thought of as 'brain exchanges'. As economies develop they require fewer hewers of wood and drawers of water and more skilled specialists. Since training these people is a long and costly business, 'importing' them from abroad is attractive. For the specialist workers the higher rewards to be gained by working overseas are a major incentive to go. Thus it is currently estimated that about 25,000 professional, technical and managerial specialists from Britain are working under contract in the Gulf states. To such contract workers can be added the many staff who work around the world for multinational organisations and for whom an overseas transfer is a normal part of their careers.

Pressure to emigrate

Pressure to emigrate is greater in those countries which have low living standards and high rates of population growth. Pressures are increased when steep gradients in standards of living occur between adjacent countries: examples in the 1950s and 1960s were the Mediterranean countries and the industrial countries of north-west Europe and today similar gradients occur between Mexico and the US, the Indian subcontinent and the Gulf states.

Specific pressures are demographic, economic, social and political. Many countries have faster population growth rates than their economies can absorb. Controls on entry in potential destination states mean that emigration cannot act as a demographic safety valve as it did in nineteenth century Europe. When West Germany stopped new labour immigration in 1973, an estimated 1.5 million Turks wishing to emigrate there were unable to do so.

High levels of unemployment and underemployment, especially in rural areas, have created pressures to emigrate as developing economies have been unable to provide work for all job-seekers. Fearful of the political consequences of a disaffected, jobless population, countries have often positively supported the emigration of their citizens, acting as recruitment agencies for employers overseas. There are social pressures to emigrate too. Family members living abroad send back information to those at home and provide assistance to those wishing to join them. Social networks are thus created which are international in scope.

Illegal migrants

An illegal migrant is someone who enters or remains in a country unlawfully. There can be very few states, except those with the most Draconian immigration legislation and enforcement, where there are not aliens whose presence contravenes the law of the state. Various terms are used to describe these people – illegal, clandestine, undocumented, irregular – but they all amount to the same thing, namely that they are staying in a foreign country without the formal permission of the state authorities to be there. It is not known how many people currently reside illegally, but studies have suggested that it could well be 15–20 million.

Illegal immigrants often exacerbate the problems governments face when formulating and operating their migration policies. During periods of economic growth illegal aliens are often tolerated, even encouraged, because they constitute a cheap and flexible labour supply. When recession occurs, attitudes change. Illegal immigrants often become scapegoats, being accused of taking the jobs of the host society, at lower pay, and being a drain on the welfare system while paying no taxes. In these circumstances it is easy to see how underground networks of communities of juridically non-existent people can be created. Such groups will inevitably be highly vulnerable, perpetually at risk of discovery and deportation.

Illegal migration results from a combination of pressure to emigrate and border controls on entry. Most illegal immigrants enter the destination legally, perhaps as students or holiday visitors, for a specified time period. When that time expires they remain and hope that they are not caught. Lacking the correct status and papers, illegal migrants are prey for unscrupulous employers and landlords, being forced to work in poor conditions and for low pay, and to live in low quality and often overcrowded accommodation.

In the past governments have sometimes turned a blind eye to illegal immigration. During the 1960s it was estimated that up to three-quarters of labour immigrants to France by-passed official channels of entry but managed to get their situations regularised afterwards.

This was due to the very strong demand for cheap immigrant labour at that time. At present the major problem of illegal migration in the world occurs between Mexico and the USA. An estimated six million Mexicans live illegally in their northern neighbour. The 1986 Immigration and Resettlement Control Act in the USA was an attempt to regularise the position of many of these.

The usual penalty for an illegal immigrant upon discovery is expulsion. Mostly this is carried out on an individual basis as discovery occurs. Occasionally, however, governments attempt to solve their problems of illegal immigration by mass expulsions, examples being half a million dispatched from Ghana in 1969 and over a million from Nigeria in 1983 and 1985. From time to time governments grant general amnesties whereby illegal immigrants who come forward have their situations regularised and are allowed to stay. In the 1970s various forms of amnesty were declared in Canada (1973), Netherlands (1975) and Australia (1976); generally these had only a limited success in that comparatively few illegals declared themselves, indicating the high level of insecurity they felt.

Illegal migration is a growing problem. With fewer states willing to take in immigrants, but with population growth in origin countries and with growing disparities in standards of living, many people migrate outside official channels. Such moves are not only between rich and poor countries; they also occur between less developed countries where only small differences in standards of living and job availability occur. Many western European countries in the early 1990s have become concerned with illegal immigrants from former Communist countries, especially Romania. Spain, Italy, Portugal and Greece are currently estimated to be playing host to $1\frac{1}{2}$–2 million illegal immigrants from the Third World, mainly Africa.

Impact at origin

The principal benefit to the countries of origin comes from the remittances and savings sent home by migrants. Remittances are monies dispatched home, usually on a regular basis, by migrants who are still abroad; savings are accumulated in the country of work and then brought home by the returning migrant. These sources of finance now form substantial proportions of the foreign earnings of many states. The use of remittances and savings varies but mostly they go to improving the lot of individual families rather than being invested in enterprises that will provide long-term benefit to the economy. One study showed that monies sent back from France to villages in the Senegal Valley were mainly used to provide day-to-day support for families left behind, and this is echoed time and again elsewhere. New houses are another popular use of remittances and many villages and towns in areas of out-migration boast new 'estates' of villas occupied by returning migrants. In agricultural areas monies from working abroad have been used to buy more land, tractors and machinery, or small businesses like shops, taxi or transport firms.

Another perceived advantage of migrating abroad has been the acquisition of useful skills that can help the origin country's economy upon return. Too often this does not happen since the skills picked up abroad do not match the employment needs of the origin countries. Often they do not require workers accustomed to highly automated factories or need large numbers of construction workers. All too frequently many of the jobs abroad done by migrants are unskilled anyway; there may even be deskilling as migrants with skills go abroad and take jobs requiring less skill but yielding higher pay than they would receive at home.

Emigration of workers has positive and negative affects on those left at home. The trauma of separation may be assuaged by the financial return. There is evidence that the economies of areas of outmigration have suffered from the absence of young adult males. These problems are especially acute in areas which have become foci of emigration, like the Kabylie in Algeria, and parts of southern Italy. Elsewhere, emigration has eased demographic pressure, as in parts of India and the Minho region of Portugal.

Impact at destination

There is overwhelming evidence that labour immigration has brought economic benefits to host countries. It has provided a means of circumventing labour shortages at low cost, thus helping to keep down wage inflation. However, in Europe particularly there has been a growing socio-economic cost as temporary migration has become permanent. Family reunion has caused rising costs in education and health provision, since the process increases the numbers of dependants. Housing has been a major problem with migrants often being forced into poor quality dwellings, often in inner city areas. In the Middle East and South Africa accommodation is provided in camps provided by employers where migrants are kept completely segregated from the local populations. In many European and North American cities labour immigration has created ghetto areas where sights, sounds and smells reflect the countries from which the populace has come – Turks in the Kreuzberg district of West Berlin, North Africans in the Goutte d'Or area of Paris, Bangladeshis in the Spitalfields area of London.

A consequence of immigration has been the rise of xenophobic attitudes on the part of the host population. At first immigrants were tolerated because they took the jobs that no one else wanted. Rising unemployment and the permanence of settlement by migrants that has become apparent have led to rising resentment, with conflict between communities and sharp political debate. For example, the French and British National Front political parties are based on the philosophy of repatriation of immigrant workers and their families.

Refugees

The estimated 15 million refugees in the world constitute a large and growing problem. Refugee movement is forced and thus distinctive from the other types of migration so far discussed in this chapter. A refugee is defined by the United Nations as someone forced to reside outside his or her own country because of a well-founded fear of persecution. In the first half of this century the refugee problem was essentially a European one. During the First World War an estimated eight million people were forcibly dislocated; the figure for the Second World War was three times greater. Resettlement of these refugees was essentially carried out in Europe, but with important groups going to the New World and Israel.

Since 1945 the refugee problem has been largely a Third World one, and has grown since large numbers of states reached independence. Today Africa has about four million refugees, mainly people fleeing from the consequences of regional wars.

Refugees present enormous problems of resettlement. Many of those involved see their position as temporary and expect to return home. Most find asylum in neighbouring states and it is not surprising that they tend to settle, often in special camps, in border areas. Where fighting continues, as in Afghanistan, these camps can easily become the focus of resistance movements from which incursions can be made. This has often led to reluctance to move away from such camps to more permanent settlements.

Within recent years the term 'economic refugee' has been applied to people seeking to move away from the abject poverty that characterises their lives. Strictly speaking they are not refugees according to the conventional definition since they do not fear persecution. In order to curb applications for asylum from those they do not consider to be real refugees, some states have passed 'carrier liability' laws.

These are designed to penalise airlines which carry passengers who do not have valid entry papers for the destination country. Since 1991, for example, the British government has been able to impose upon airlines a fine of £2000 for every unauthorised passenger arrival.

Events in the Middle East in 1990 illustrate again that a 'refugee crisis' can spring up seemingly out of nowhere. In the unlikely event of no major new sources of refugees becoming important, the resettlement of existing refugees already poses a stiff challenge to all countries.

Project Work

The exercises suggested here fall into two categories. The first is based on 'local' information, provided by members of your study group, either from their own experiences or from local field sources. The second relies upon standard sources of statistical data which should be readily accessible in institutional and local public libraries.

Local studies

1 Gather information about migration by asking members of your study group about moves made by their families over the last five years. Distinguish between moves made in the last year and moves made over the whole period. Note the distance moved, the assumed reasons for the moves and any other relevant information. How do these moves fit into the various types of migration discussed in the book?

2 From information on the birth-places of the members of your group, produce a graph of the distances moved between their births and the present day. Do the results fit the idea of a gravity model discussed in the book?

3 Put together a series of longitudinal studies of migration by gathering information over a long time period of the moves made by class members, by their parents and by their grandparents. Do any repetitive patterns emerge? How do the various moves you have recorded fit into the classification of migration discussed in this book?

4 From the information available from members of your class undertake studies of special groups, for example siblings who have left home for higher education or elderly family members who have moved on retirement. Examine such details as the distance they moved, their choice of destination, and reasons for their decision to move.

5 Conduct a field survey of the inhabitants of a new housing estate, where all the residents will be migrants of some kind or other. Design your own questions, but focus on distance of move, occupational type and reasons for moving.

6 Search local and national newspapers for a week and pick out those stories which are connected with the process of population migration (new housing, immigration, refugees, labour migration, etc). How have the newspapers dealt with these issues (for example sympathetically, antagonistically, stressing social implications, stressing economic implications, etc)? Does any pattern emerge in the attitudes that are

shown to different kinds of migration?

7 Undertake field studies in a local urban area to observe and, if possible, map evidence of distinctive immigrant groups. Examples would be specialist shops, religious buildings, distinctive decorations on houses, etc. To what extent does this evidence point to the presence of one or a number of different ethnically-distinctive groups?

Data-based studies

8 Using the population census volumes extract information on the distance moved and the socio-economic group of migrants. Cross-tabulate different variables; for example, do members of certain occupations move further than others? Also compare the migration experience of different regions. In Britain data may be obtained at the national level in *National Migration (GB), parts I and II* (Cen 81 MS Series) and at a local authority level in *Regional Migration* (Cen 81 RM Series). Both are published by HMSO for the Office of Population Censuses and Surveys.

9 Use census data to produce a matrix of gains and losses of population between regions as a result of migration. Distinguish between net and gross flows.

10 Compare patterns of in-movement and out-movement for particular cities, looking especially at the distances involved.

11 Use data on migration and rates of natural population change (i.e. as a result of birth and death rates) to produce a map showing components of change. Select various places which you think are contrasting on general geographical grounds (for example, seaside resorts, old industrial cities, new towns) and see if there are any contrasts in the underlying causes of population change. The data may be found in Census County Reports, Table 3. This source gives intercensal change by 'births and deaths' (i.e. natural change) and 'balance' (i.e. migration).

12 Use the data on international migration, published annually in Britain by the Office of Population Censuses and Surveys, to calculate and graph trends in international migration to and from Great Britain. The data may be obtained from *International Migration*, an annual volume from the Office of Population Censuses and Surveys (Series NM).

13 Using the same source, analyse immigration and emigration in terms of the characteristics of migrants (for example nationality, age, sex, socio-economic group).

14 Using the same (or some similar) source, calculate the balance of international migration between the UK (or any other country for which data are available) and other countries or regions (such as the European Community, 'Old' Commonwealth countries, 'New' Commonwealth etc.).

Bibliography and further reading

A highly useful book which expands many of the topics covered here is:

P. Ogden, 1984, *Migration and Geographical Change*, Cambridge University Press.

A more advanced volume which contains a series of specialist essays is:

P. White and R. Woods (eds), 1980, *The Geographical Impact of Migration*, Longman.

For the brief perspective of a sociologist on some of the themes discussed here see:

J.A. Jackson, 1986, *Migration* (Aspects of Modern Sociology Series), Longman.

A Third World dimension to population movement is found in some of the chapters of:

A. Gilbert and J. Gugler, 1982, *Cities, Poverty and Development: Urbanization in the Third World*, Oxford University Press.

For migration in the context of Europe see:

S Castles, H. Booth and T. Wallace, 1984, Here for Good. Western Europe's New Ethnic Minorities, Pento.

For a recent view of labour migration see:

J.H. Johnson and J. Salt (eds), 1990, *Labour Migration: The Internal Mobility of Labour in the Developed World*, D. Fulton.

An economic view of immigration, dealing mostly with the United States is:

J. Simon, 1989, *The Economic Consequences of Immigration*, Blackwell.

Probably the best book on refugees is:

A.R. Zolberg, A. Suhrke and S. Aguayo, 1989, *Escape from Violence*, Oxford University Press.

Various pieces of work which are referred to specifically in the text are:

H. Jones, 1990, Population Geography, P. Chapman.

W. Zelinsky, 1971, 'The hypothesis of the mobility transition', Geographical Review 61, 219–49.

L. Brown and E. Moore, 1970, 'The intra-urban migration process: a perspective', Geografiska Annaler 52B, 1–13.

S. Kennett, 1977, 'Migration within and between metropolitan economic labour areas in Britain, 1966–71', in J. Hobcraft and P. Rees (eds), Regional Demographic Development, Croom Helm.

R. Flowerdew and J. Salt, 1979, 'Migration between labour market areas in Great Britain, 1970–71', Regional Studies 13, 211–31.

A. Warnes and C. Law, 1984, 'The elderly population of Great Britain: locational trends and policy implications', Transactions of the Institute of British Geographers 9, 37–59.

J. H. Johnson, J. Salt and P. Wood, 1974, Housing and the Migration of Labour in England and Wales, Saxon House.

SOPEMI, 1990, Continuous reporting system on Migration, OECD.

J. S. Birks, I. J. Seccombe and C. A. Sinclair, 1988, 'Labour migration in the Arab Gulf States: patterns, trends and prospects', International Migration 26, 267–86.